FAITH AND SPECULATION

FAITH AND SPECULATION

An Essay in Philosophical Theology

containing
The Deems Lectures
1964

AUSTIN FARRER

T. & T. CLARK
EDINBURGH

Copyright © 1967 Austin Farrer
Original U.K. edition published by A. & C. Black Ltd. London 1967.

Printed and bound in the U.K. by Page Bros Ltd, Norwich,

for

T. & T. CLARK LTD,
59 George Street, Edinburgh EH2 2LQ

First printed 1988.

British Library Cataloguing in Publication Data
Farrer, Austin
Faith and speculation: an essay in philosophical theology:
containing the Deems lectures 1964.
1. Religion—Philosophy
I. Title
200'.1   BL51
ISBN 0–567–29141–3

PREFACE

This book is a continuous reflection on theistic belief, in its double aspect of working faith and rational conviction. The discussion develops out of itself, moving on from a consideration of the religious phenomenon into suggestions for the revision of philosophical theology.

I have no doubt written too many books; but I have not stated anything like a position in rational theology for a score of years. I find myself identified with every thesis I put forward in the 40's of the century; and I have no right to complain, unless I give a more up-to-date account of myself.

An essay, especially a short essay, might be expected to deal with a single topic, and to attack it in a workmanlike manner. It is a shame that I cannot state in three words the subject of this book. In the autumn of 1964 I had the honour of delivering the Deems Lectures in the University of New York, taking for my title 'the conceivability of a divine action in the world'. I set myself to illustrate the paradox of double agency, divine and creaturely, in the three fields of Grace, Nature, and History; and to show that so far from being a speculative embarrassment, the paradox involved is the form of practical religious thinking. The substance of those lectures appears in chapters IV–VI of the present work. I have led into them with an empirical approach to the fact of religious existence; and have added after them a working out of resultant pragmatic considerations in certain topics of metaphysical theology. In these final chapters I take occasion to purge out the old Aristotelian leaven from the voluntarist metaphysics I sketched so many years ago in *Finite and Infinite*.

I hope my readers will have patience with the discursive

method of my essay. I wish I had written the book better; I do not wish I had written it more formally. Reflection and discussion may permit realities to disclose themselves to us; and I would rather, if I dared to hope it, provide materials for an exercise in understanding, than formalise a chain of argument.

My thanks are due to the University of New York for honouring me with the Deems Lectureship and for all the kindness shown me on the occasion of my visit. Among the many philosophical friends who have given me food for thought I will mention Dr Diogenes Allen of Princeton, and Professor John Glasse of Vassar. The latter persuaded me to do the rethinking of scholastic positions which runs through my seventh, eighth and ninth chapters; the former I have plundered in my first.

OXFORD, *July* 1966

CONTENTS

CHAPTER I

THE BELIEVER'S REASONS

RIGHTLY or wrongly, the contemporary mind sees something almost comic in the old rational theology. We find it absurd that anyone should pretend to discount both the fact and the form of religious belief, while he rakes the universe for signs of a First Cause. One might as well start an examination of the Iliad by discounting any acceptance of it as written language, and take the marks on the pages as sheer phenomena, caused by—caused by what? That would be the question. Whereas we know perfectly well that but for the accepted position of the Iliad as an important poem no one would be bothering with it in the way the learned do. Since it is so striking an epic, we want to know whether it is a single composition, whether any of it is historically true, whether its occasional obscurities can be clarified. Otherwise we should not care. And so with theistic belief. The belief is of human importance; that is why the philosophical enquirer is moved to ask whether all or any of it is well grounded, and what its more mysterious assertions mean.

Is not the pretence of any other starting-point the pretence of jumping off one's own shadow? How could we possibly escape from the cultural history of our race? How experience the theistic suggestiveness of the world, as we might have done if there had never been theology? How experiment with an uninterpreted environment, to see whether it prompts the formation of a brand-new interpretative concept, the concept—dear me, yes!—the concept of God? Whatever the rational theologian may pretend to do, he will in fact be considering a question posed to him by religious belief; and he may as well be aboveboard about it.

But if a neutral approach to the grand question involves a fiction, there is fiction equally to be guarded against in an approach from the side of religious conviction. What is the philosopher's programme to be? Taking the conviction as human fact, he is to look into the grounds that might justify it. But in what field is he to look for them? Surely in the field of religious thought. The philosopher's concern is whether any theology is true. But if it is true, it will not surely be true by accident; it will be true because the grounds or motives for such belief have been sound. So it is actual motives or grounds for religious believing which demand the philosopher's attention.

So far, so good. But at this point the philosopher is tempted to bring in *mal à propos* a philosophical stock-position. A belief that has grounds is a belief formed and held in response to the pressure of perceived facts. No doubt (he may say) there can be many motives of a non-cognitive kind for paying attention to a belief, or for elaborating it; this is so, for example, in the case of scientific doctrines. An interest in bridging rivers is a motive for considering and perfecting hypotheses about the structural properties of steel; but ascertained fact is the only basis for believing any doctrine about the tensile properties of that material. And similarly the Christian's desire to attain salvation or to find an overall meaning in existence may be a respectable enough motive for his bothering with religion; it cannot be a justifiable motive for his believing it.

If then (the philosopher continues) religious believers are not to admit that their belief is groundless, they are bound to claim for the religious mind a cognitive activity leading to the formation of the basic religious concepts; an activity which appreciates certain facts or qualities among things ʼand interprets them by the concepts it is led to form.

The conclusion seems very reasonably drawn; but so much the worse for the premises which yield it. For it lands us in a fiction. Believers offer no such account of their basic thinking, nor can they commonly be brought to an awareness of ever having done what is thus attributed to them. Badgered by philosophers, and led through the steps of argument we have just set out, the Christian may indeed be induced to postulate what he cannot observe. 'Since my faith has all the force of objectivity' he says to himself, 'I suppose I must do (or have done) what alone could make it objective, even though I have no awareness of doing so. Yes, as I go about I must perceive the God-suggestive aspects of things and on the basis of my perceptions accept or formulate the theology which they alone can justify.'

But after making such a speech to himself the believer, if he is a reflective or critical man, must remain somewhat mystified. The Bourgeois Gentilhomme was happy to be informed that he had talked prose all his life, without knowing it; and there is much information of a like character which common men accept from philosophers with an equal complacency. We shall not so easily convince M. Jourdain that he has talked all his life in rhyming couplets—has lisped in numbers, while knowing only that he lisped. And when the believer is told to claim objective perceptions of God-suggestive qualities, he does not feel that he is simply being given an acceptable analysis of admitted experiences or procedures on his part. He feels more like the man whom to his great surprise we inform at breakfast that he has been round the garden asleep in his night clothes. 'But you must have been round; you picked a dozen roses and put them in the rose-bowl.'—'Goodness me! and there the roses are. I suppose I must have.' So the presence of the firm convictions in a believer's mind is made the evidence of his having been through the beds of experience from which alone he could have gathered them; and if he has not done so when he was awake to it, then presumably he did so when he was asleep to it.

The believer may be pardoned if he suspects that the roses got into the bowl—that is, the convictions into his head—by some other channel. Nor does there seem to be any difficulty in hitting upon it. How did religion get into our heads? It was taught to us, was it not? Even if we were reared in atheistic ignorance, we became acquainted with the faith before we were converted to it. And however far back you go, it is the same story. You might think that you would reach an absolute beginning somewhere—Someone taught, not because he had been taught, but because he discovered. In fact we come to no such beginning in recorded time. Many teachers have taught things they had not themselves been taught; Christ, for example, and Moses. But the novelty was never religion itself. The pioneer began with a hereditary system for interpreting things religiously, and in doing so found himself driven to innovation in religion—not to an innovation called 'religion'.

There is no great mystery, then, about the source from which any given generation of believers derives the key-concepts of religion. It is to be found in tradition or history, not in a subliminal annex to the philosophy of cognition. Very well; but a historical explanation leaves untouched the philosopher's concern for objective truth. The historical explanation of an idea satisfies us, if the idea gives shape to a harmless custom in matters indifferent, which we are content to follow; or if it constitutes a superstition which we are ready to discard. But if it claims to express truth or to determine right, the question is not whence it came, but why we should accept it; and the second question cannot be answered by merely answering the first. Common experience keeps the distinction before our attention; for while you can indoctrinate children with a religious tradition, you cannot keep adolescents in it, unless they come to find it intrinsically convincing. They need to appreciate religion as something which 'works' for themselves and for others, however they may suppose it to 'work', whether as a principle of interpretation, or as a power for good.

Once a historical tradition is appreciated for giving us something which 'works', our attitude to its historical venerability takes the colour of our present experience. We are impressed to observe how long, and under what a variety of conditions, that which works for us appears to have worked for others. At the same time we cannot be blind to the modifications or developments which the tradition has sustained. Whatever was its original form, it has been continually knocked into shape by the pressures of existence. It has been retained because it works, it has been changed so as to work better.

When we have reached this point, we can afford to disinterest ourselves in the question of historical origins; it loses all philosophical importance. I can only blush now to remember with what heat I disputed some years ago against a philosophical atheist. I maintained that belief in deity was 'natural' and so arose spontaneously the world over when men attained a certain level of intellectual cultivation. He maintained that it was simply a bad idea which happened to occur to somebody somewhere; it had spread all over the earth because it was the useful support of another dubious invention, sacred chieftainship. I should no longer wish to take sides in this debate, except by way of mere historical speculation. For all I can see, my opponent and I might perfectly well have swapped positions without either of us gaining or losing an inch of ground.

To take his case first. Is belief in deity a stupid error? Then it could perfectly well be suggested independently to stupid minds placed in similar circumstances; and the more stupid you think it, the less difficulty should you have in supposing that many minds should independently hit upon it; for dullness is common. And now to take my case. Is the theological idea natural to man, as expressing the truth of his condition? But it is not natural to apes, nor can it have been so to our apelike progenitors. The 'man' to whom it is natural can only be the man who has reached a certain level of mental culture, and there is no reason *a priori*—still less *a posteriori*—for supposing the rise in cultural level to have been everywhere uniform and contemporaneous. Why should not a single tribe have pioneered the religious development?

Articulate speech may fairly be reckoned the foundation of the mentality we call distinctively human. What difficulty (other than the evidence afforded by surviving languages) can attach to the supposition that the decisive advance from grunts to sentences was itself the achievement of a single group, and spread

5

by general imitation? The tribe which invented speech might be fairly said to have invented human nature. The position I thought I was defending against my atheist was that something like theistic belief is natural to the talking animal. But I could not mean that as soon as they talked grammar they talked theology. The most I could claim would be that if the talking beast continued to talk, he would be bound to talk himself into religion at last. I could not hope to dogmatise on the time it would take him; nor preclude the possibility that the decisive step should be achieved by one tribal group, and picked up by others before they thought of it for themselves. For the 'naturalness' of religious belief cannot be supposed to lie in its spontaneous occurrence to all individuals, but only in its acceptability to men in general, never mind who first thought of it, whether one person or several.

Whatever the origins of theological belief, it is propagated by communication; but since humanity itself is so propagated, the fact raises no particular scandal. We can have small interest in asserting that men are more naturally religious than they are naturally human; and children are born potentially human, that is all; they are smiled and talked into being actually so. Children are also talked and loved into religious belief. They can be reckoned to have been already potential believers, if it is of any interest to anyone to advance on their behalf so shadowy a claim. You might not think so. Yet as a matter of history, a passionate interest has been felt in what looks like the same issue. Are human beings by birth 'the children of God', or does their religious initiation make them so? Perhaps the issue would cease to generate theological heat, if its philosophical bearings were more clearly appreciated.

It is time we called a halt to what is surely a digression. Prehistory is not our present business. All that can concern us is a bare generalisation. Religion, like much other lore, is taught us. Being taught us, it does, or does not, continue to hold us. If we want to judge whether it should, we must scrutinise the motives it evokes in those it continues to hold, and see whether they are adequate to justify belief.

At this point of my exposition I see as out of the tail of my eye the knitted brow of the philosophical critic bent upon me. 'You dismissed me ten minutes ago' he says, 'cavalierly enough. You objected to my introducing what you called a philosophical stock-position, or determining *a priori* the sort of grounds which would justify theological tenets. You recommended a more docile and accommodating approach, attending to the motives of belief which are actually operative. Very well. But you do not, I take it, simply propose an empirical enquiry. You are not content to establish biographical facts about believing individuals, or psychological facts about believing types. You are well aware that men have persisted in faith for illogical, inadequate or frankly unworthy reasons. You want to see whether any of their reasons are justifying reasons. In fact, you want to separate the sheep from the goats—if it turns out that there are any sheep. How, then, would you know a sheep if you saw one? That is, by what criterion would you judge a motive of belief to be a genuine ground for that belief? All your goats are *ex hypothesi* disguised in sheep's clothing—all motives present themselves as respectable motives. How will you make the necessary distinction? Will you not have to readmit at this point the philosophical stock-position you previously excluded? For what can your criterion be, if it is not the criterion universally applicable to the grounds of existential assertion—that they must present, or must indicate, ostensible facts calling for such an assertion?'

Our answer to our critic's proposal is a modest request for a little more patience. If it were obvious where the experiential evidence for religious beliefs is to be sought, or how it comes to bear in determining belief, we could get down to our philosophical criticism without delay. But it is notorious that these points are by no means clear, and that *a priori* approaches to them by impatient philosophers have helped little. And so it seems better to start from the way believers think, feel and decide. Now believers themselves search their hearts and criticise their own motives; they have their own criteria for distinguishing a sound motive of faith from a rotten one. Before we come in with our philosophical yardstick, it will be prudent to observe how they handle theirs. We will continue to take as our typical believer a Christian brought up in the simple acceptance of his faith, grown up into an awareness of many reasons taken to discredit belief, but still persistent in believing. What is his motive? We may make all sorts of suppositions. Perhaps his impressionable youth has been played upon by a spiritual charlatan hawking fake miracles. Here is a ground of belief which all honest believers will condemn as worthless, once the imposture is known; the dupe himself, once disabused, will concur. He may, of course, decide that the discreditable influence played a purely accidental part in his spiritual history. It jerked him back into a belief which justified itself on more intrinsic grounds. If so, he will continue to believe; but he will nevertheless repudiate the imposture as a ground for faith.

Acceptance of imposture is a clear example of bad grounds for belief. It is clear, because it is extreme; but because it is extreme, it is scarcely typical. The invalid motives more commonly suspected or imputed are subjective. For example, emotional compensation—those who cannot win the affection or esteem of their fellows like to see themselves the favourites of heaven. Another is evasion of responsibility—a passive acquiescence in divine directives excuses from the effort of decision. A third is cushioning from painful truth—a pious fairy-tale stands substitute for a harsh reality. Last and perhaps worst is the desire to replace practical virtue by ritual fuss.

Here is a list of motives for belief which the honest believer will repudiate or condemn. But, if he is intellectually alert, he will be anxious to make quite clear what it is that he condemns or repudiates. For he will know that, under cover of attacking such unworthy motives, an unsympathetic tongue may assail the most precious grounds of faith. Divine love is not to be made a substitute for human charities, no; but it is the ultimate consolation, the ultimate felicity; and if the inevitable disappointments of human affection turn the creature towards the Creator, the lesson of life has been wisely learnt. Docility in face of spiritual authority may be the resort of moral cowardice. But on the other hand the brave and open mind which finds frustration in ungrounded choice and accepts the divine will as the condition of freedom, shows the discretion which is the better part of valour. To substitute a pious fairytale for the stern realities of existence is the most pitiful deception; but to find the true colour of goods and evils in their relation to divine purpose is a vital illumination. Worship is not to be substituted for practical virtue, no; but practical virtue finds its orientation in a life of worship.

The moral of these antitheses is plain. In the view of the believer, the more insidious bad motives of belief are the twins, shadows and parodies of corresponding good motives. The bad motives are negatives, impoverishments of existence, starvings of the soul, exclusions from that very grace of God which they claim to embrace. The good motives are positives, enrichments, nourishments, enlivenings. Men who see that they believe for such reasons feel no cause for self-reproach.

'Admittedly they do not' it may be rejoined 'but that only shows that they are not philosophers. If they are right in what they claim, the personal advantages of a believing attitude are palpable. But surely none of them is a good reason for believing. Why may not a metaphysical delusion have certain psychologically wholesome effects? To support the hypothesis of a Personal First Cause you need factual evidence of a sort which none of the happy considerations you have listed can supply.'

What will a believer say after subjection to such a cold douche of philosophy as this is? Will he say 'Dear me, yes, you are perfectly right. When I was distinguishing good from bad motives of belief I was wasting my time. Some of them may have expressed more amiable attitudes than others but, as motives for belief, they were all equally disreputable'?

It is indeed possible that, chivvied by philosophers, the believing innocent might make such an admission; but surely he neither need nor should. Let us gift the man with a little more discretion, and let him try again. 'What you urge,' he now says to the philosopher 'sounds very convincing and I don't know how to answer it direct. But then I do not think along the sort of lines you seem to follow and so I find it difficult to come to grips with you. I dare say the way I do think will seem to you extremely silly, but what is the use of my being bashful about it? Well then—the Christian faith was preached to me as a gospel of salvation. Perhaps—though I do not know—the credal propositions it contains might be verified along various other and more scientific lines, but I cannot claim to have tried any line but one—the line directly suggested by the claim of the gospel to be a gospel. It offers to me the blessing of a union of will with the primal Will. I follow the way of union which it prescribes and I find that the blessing blesses. There is the fundamental blessing of finding oneself where one belongs and there are the consequent blessings such as those we were listing just now. The gospel offers God to me as good, not simply as fact. In embracing the good I am convinced of the fact.'[1]

'I can only thank you' replies the philosopher 'for so frank an avowal. So far as an outsider can judge, you are telling the truth about the Christian attitude. For your words tally with the direct language of piety as I see it expressed in hymns, prayers and other effusions of the kind. But the avowal that you make only serves to pinpoint the philosophical difficulty; the difficulty of establishing the existence of an utterly unique reality by experiencing the comfort of an attitude of faith towards it. And so, if it is not inhuman of me, I should like to press you a little further; if perhaps you could examine your thoughts, and tell me your reasons for holding, not that the faith-attitude is a blessing, but that the object of faith is an existent being.'

'It is not at all inhuman' replies his believing friend, 'to press me for such explanations—not inhuman in the least, but merely hopeless. You see, I am no philosopher, and since I have never asked myself philosophical questions, I have no philosophical answers to offer. You are raising a philosophical difficulty which,

[1] For a careful exposition of the believer's sufficient reasons, see Dr D. Allen, *American Philosophical Quarterly*, April 1966.

I am sure, is perfectly real. I take it to be the business of philosophers to strip the mask of uncritical assumption from the face of experience, to raise and to solve problems of which common-sense is unaware. For example, it is an intriguing question to philosophers, how we men know one another's minds and appreciate one another's feelings. But it is a question to philosophers only. The rest of us take it as fact that we know our neighbours in dealing with them; we trust the mechanism of perception or interpretation, whatever it may be, to do its work, without attempting to take it to pieces. And so, if philosophy asks us what reason we have for supposing that we know our neighbours, we have no answer for her except a confession of ignorance. We have no reasons for it, because we have always taken it for granted. You might as well ask us how we suppose that we can move our hands by an act of will. We don't suppose; we get on with it. In the same way we go on in our religion, taking it for granted that the founding, steadying, invigorating, illumining and enriching of our existence which we find in it, is the action of the God to whom we pray; and who, it appears, extends a similar beneficent action to our fellow-believers.

'Please don't misunderstand me' (this unphilosophical Christian continues). 'I have no objection whatever to the philosophical question's being raised. On the contrary, I am bound to think that the answering of it, if it can be answered, will cast a fascinating light on the cause of the world and the whole pattern of existence. But you are asking me for the motives of my belief. And what is the use of my pretending to find them in answers to philosophical questions—questions which I have never had the wit or the will to formulate? I assume God's existence in relating my life to him; and the question I ask is not, how truly God corresponds to my idea of him; it is "What shall I do to be saved?" Any more than I asked at the time of my marriage whether my wife was truly what I took her to be, but whether she was the woman for me. You can say if you like that by marrying her I made an act of faith in the practical reliability attaching to my idea of her; but I had no notion I was doing it. I was putting my faith in the constancy of her character, not in the soundness of my cognitive process.

'You need not exclaim at the naivety of a comparison between relation with a fellow-being and relation with one's Creator. I am well aware of the vast difference. But the difference, so far from weakening my practical argument, strengthens it. I can be assured of my neighbour's mere existence quite apart from the pursuit of a personal relation with him: if I want to be sure that he is a speaking animal I can pinch him. I can make no such gross experiments on my Creator. I can only approach him through religious attention to him and see whether the good promised in his name is forthcoming from his hand.'

We have allowed the believer and his critic to speak at some length. We will break off here and strike the balance of the debate. The philosophical enquiry into the grounds for belief in God is neither an examination of the reasons which lead the believer into commitment, nor is it an independent investigation unrelated to those reasons. It is an examination of an assumption which, in accepting those reasons, the believer makes.

From this position there follows a corollary. The believer's account of his faith is neither a philosophical vindication of its correctness, nor a philosophical disclosure of its groundlessness. He has motives for his belief; and the adequacy of these motives (even granting the general assumption on which they rest) can be both attacked and defended. But then, further, he proceeds on an assumption; and the assumption can itself be both questioned and supported. His belief is not shown to be groundless by the mere fact that he has never questioned his general assumption. We could not get on with life in any province unless we were entitled to 'natural' assumptions, which we take to be the proper functioning of a sound mentality. If all thinking based on uncriticised assumption is groundless, then all thinking is groundless. But what is not groundless may still be ill-grounded; and when philosophical criticism develops it will torture every assumption it has the ability to isolate or define. Meanwhile the believer, convinced of the reality of what he handles, is entitled to the confidence that his gold will never be proved dross by logical acid.

The position we have been outlining indicates a starting-point for the philosopher who approaches the theological question. His task is to see whether the believer's experience of salvation or fulfilment in his embracing of an apparent divine Good can intelligibly justify his assumption that the blessings which accrue are the work of actual deity. But to mark the starting-point is not to limit the field of enquiry. The philosopher who attempts the question from the angle we have suggested will be excused none of the topics belonging to traditional discussion. The appeal to the experienced, or to the existential, may often wear the mask of a fallacious simplicity. 'It is just a matter of deciding whether the Godgivenness of life is truly experienced by those who claim to experience it.'—'It is just a matter of deciding whether existence does or doesn't become uniquely authentic by relation to the divine.' Such formulas let us off nothing, philosophically speaking. It still has to be shown that 'the God-givenness of life' is anything more than a rhetorical expression about the feel of life itself; and that 'the divine by relation to which existence is authentic' is anything else than a figure in our brains. If the God whose name comes into our simple questions is meant as a creative omnipotence, it has to be shown that the universe of finites allows of being interpreted as his creation, and so forth. Every one of the old problems remains. Except, you may say, the proof of God from the world. At least we are rid of that. Are we? I do not think so. Can you argue that the finites *allow* of being read as creations of the Infinite, without arguing that they *ask* to be read as such? How can the finites even allow of dependence upon an Infinite, unless it is in virtue of an existential insufficiency which requires such a dependence? And so we shall be obliged to examine the case for the demonstration *a contingentia mundi*, after all. We may let ourselves off the claim that the force of the proof is evident to an unbelieving mind. We can say if we like that the existential insufficiency of the finites is imperceptible apart from awareness of the Infinite, and that such an awareness comes through faith. What we cannot (I suspect) say is that the finites could as well have been uncreated, for anything we can ever see in them; but that they just do happen to have been created by God, for faith assures us of it.

In the desultory dialogue which has formed the substance of this chapter, we have allowed philosophy and religious belief to personify themselves in separate characters. Historically speaking, this is a falsification. Most philosophers have been believers, however unorthodox; and few believers capable of conversing with philosophers have been innocent of philosophy, however puerile. Any writer who wishes to make out a handsome case for orthodoxy seems bound to take as his norm the mind in which an entire faith is balanced by a luminous philosophical wisdom. But though the believer and the philosopher may reside in the same bosom, a certain importance attaches to the sorting-out of their several activities. The believer believes a gospel and the assurance of his faith lies in his embracing it. If he is a reflective man he philosophises, most likely in a quite second-hand way, about the implications of his faith and about the assumptions on which it rests. It may well be that if he could not philosophise his position at all he would be driven to relinquish his faith; and fairly enough, since his faith claims to be true and therefore to find a thinkable place in the whole body of accepted truth. So, by his philosophising, he both expresses and maintains his belief. Nevertheless his philosophising may be exceedingly bad. It must be open to endless correction, and the correction must be a technical job, whatever else it may be besides.

The importance of a proper distinction between saving faith and philosophical reflection lies here. No progress is possible so long as it is supposed that faith is or contains an elementary, or an implicit, or any other sort of philosophy which believers are bound to defend, since upon it their confidence reposes. No doubt believers will inevitably become attached to their philosophical positions and spread over them the vesture of sanctity;

as the late Middle Age canonised an Aristotelian cosmology which was basically pagan. They are to be persuaded nevertheless that their vitals are not being torn away when their philosophy is jettisoned; as misers may learn that they can lose their gold without losing their souls; or as limpets may be detached from rocks without leaving their flesh adhering.

But if a proper distinction of saving faith from pious philosophy is vital, equally vital is a just relation between them. Otherwise the philosopher loses his starting-point. He must know that he is examining or articulating the assumptions of the believing mind.

CHAPTER II

THE EMPIRICAL DEMAND

In our previous chapter the empiricist, ready armed with his criterion for truths of fact, attempted once and again to foreclose, and each time he was put off. He was to wait until it became clear just what it was he had to test; once that had become clear, he was (for anything we said) to do the testing on his own terms and by his own methods. But surely this was mere temporising. However long the believer is given to explain himself, and at whatever point the test is applied, a strict empirical criterion for truth of fact must condemn theistic belief. So much is evident *a priori* and in advance of any experiment's being made. If the case for belief is to be given a serious hearing, two conditions must be fulfilled, not one. Not only must the actual structure of believing thought be allowed free deployment; the question must also be raised, what refinement of the empirical principle could conceivably square with the validity of the thought-structure thus deployed. Only then would follow the assessment: 'Is the empirical principle, so stretched as to cover the theological *genre*, still of any substance? And will it, even so, allow this or that theological assertion?'

To turn back from the assessment to the two conditions, or preliminaries it requires; the first of them was, however perfunctorily, handled in our previous chapter; of the second nothing has been said. We have done something towards deploying the structure of belief; we have still to rack the empirical principle.

Before we begin, it may be as well to take warning from sorrowful experience. What commonly happens when the issue of theology and empiricism is raised? The empiricist points out that his criterion for factual statements, however stretched, will not allow a truth-claim to theological assertions. The believer retorts that anyone who scanned theological assertions with half an eye could see that the empirical criterion is inapplicable to them; you might as well measure yards with a stop-watch or minutes with a foot-rule.

The upshot of the exchange is purely negative. A hopeful bridge has been broken down, that is all. It seemed as though there ought to be some analogy between assertions about God and assertions about finite subjects. We were mistaken, there is none; or anyhow, if there is, we have not discovered where it lies. It is theology that feels the discredit of our failure. For theology makes assertions about a supposedly real subject. The subject is admittedly unique, and (as I have heard an eminent Frenchman say) uniquely unique. Nevertheless if the assertion made about this subject cannot find a place, however singular, in the family of assertions about undeniably real subjects, we shall wonder whether it asserts anything.

Theology, then, should not evade any just claim of the empirical demand. But what is the empirical demand? It is the well-known paradox of philosophical history, that a principle which obtained its prestige from the development of physical science should have been defined by our over-praised English philosophers in a sense inapplicable to scientific practice. Science is not, as Berkeley and Hume might lead you to suppose, the codification of recurrent uniformities in the pattern of our sense-data. The scientist, like every sane animal since animal life began, takes the signs his five senses offer as revelatory of environmental blocks or environmental forces with which he can or must interact. Seeing is believing, but contact is knowledge. Physics is not concerned with the way things look but with the way they act; and the method of physical discovery is physical interference. As knowledge arises from interference, so it issues in control. We are hardly said physically to understand a process which we can neither stimulate, direct, modify nor neutralise. Not that we can do much about the revolutions of the planets;

but then we theorise them as cases of a physical motion which, in suitable models, is perfectly subject to experiment.

The relation of physical knowledge to physical manipulation is yet more intimate than this. Not only is the manipulation the condition of the knowledge; the knowledge is inextricable from the manipulation. Environmental agencies or forces are known to us in and through their interaction with us. It is quite rightly the scientific ideal to abstract them from it and state them purely as they are in themselves. The ideal may be approached, but is for ever unrealisable. We make our statements as objective as we can, but the most objective statement is never perfectly so.

Now what is empiricism? It is spoken of as the banner of a party, as though there were forces of antiempiricism for empiricists to fight. Where, then, is the debatable country? Is the rough sketch of physical method which we have just given an empiricist, or an antiempiricist story? How could it be either one or the other? Is it not the simple generalisation of familiar facts? Who, without self-stultification, can contest it? The battle used at one time to rage over the universality of the laws our science claimed to establish. Was our conviction of nature's perfect law-abidingness a postulate of Reason or a generalisation from fact? Were the fundamental laws of physics hypotheses justified by evidence, or were they intrinsic intelligible necessities? Those who threw the weight on the side of observation or experiment were empiricists; their opponents, the a-priorists or rationalists, emphasised the independent and sovereign deliverances of pure Reason. What has become of the grand old battle? it is still possible, perhaps, to incline a little one way or the other on the issue; it can no longer be dressed up as a life-and-death affair. It is no more than a matter of defining, at a particular point, the relativity of our knowledge to our activity. We shall all agree that there must be actual uniformities in natural processes, for otherwise we could not codify them as we do. We shall equally agree that the codes themselves are linguistic forms constructed by us, according to logical rules which we find either necessary or convenient. The depth of mental colour, the degree of diagrammatic fiction, thus inevitably introduced into our picture of nature, may be variously estimated. The variety of our estimates no longer places us in mutually opposed camps. No reasonable thinker who inclines to emphasise the mental or linguistic factor deserves to be labelled 'a-priorist' or 'rationalist'; so why should an inclination to the other side justify the boast of being empiricist?

The frontier is now elsewhere. It no longer runs between the factors in physical knowledge, but between physical knowledge as such and other areas of cognition. The empiricist wishes to see the line drawn as lightly as possible; that is, he would like to see anything that could fairly be called knowledge of fact or of existence brought into the closest possible approximation to physical knowledge. No one of course denies the visible differences which distinguish personal knowledge on a commonsense level, not to mention historical knowledge of a reconstructed past, from physical science, or physical acquaintance. Nevertheless the empiricist philosopher interprets in every field by means of a logic obtained by abstraction from physical method; which means in practice that nothing passes as knowledge of fact except in so far as it can be accommodated to the scientific model, or the scientific model accommodated to it.

It is easy to write off such an empiricism as the prejudice of fashion. When was there not a tendency among philosophers to treat some single branch of science as the model of all organised knowledge? The schools of Plato and Aristotle, all the way down to Leibniz and Locke, made the mathematics their typical sciences, of which all others were broken-down analogies, or imperfect copies: a view which now seems so fantastic, we wonder it could have held the field for a moment; so plain does it appear that pure mathematics afford us no knowledge of anything, being but the systematic elaboration of a linguistic instrument. But are we any wiser, when we elevate physics into the throne from which we have pulled the mathematics down? Is she the queen of knowledge? Must all other claimants to factual truth or even significance be judged by their likeness to the royal face? What if the analogy they bear to her is handled with the greatest sensitivity, in accommodation to their special and various characteristics? The disciples of Aristotle were often most flexible in the business of extending their mathematical analogy. Their method was vicious, all the same. Why should we imagine the most liberal physicalism to be any less so?

Why, indeed? But to dethrone the usurper is a purely negative operation; and anarchy is a result we cannot tolerate. The philosophical mind cannot happily accept separate branches of knowledge, without relating them to any root principle. Can we believe that several sorts of thinking express truth of fact, or of existence, without any common structure running through them all? That nothing can be said in general about the logic, by which thought or speech in several provinces shapes itself upon the realities it claims to disclose?

What, then, are we to do? Is there not work here for an infinite patience, and an encyclopedic learning? There can surely be no short cuts. If we want to trace the articulation of the one cognitive activity through its various branches, we have a formidable task. We must examine the logic of the mind's procedure in each branch severally, we must compare our findings, and we must construct from them such generalisations as we are able to formulate. The programme, however daunting, has been a traditional exercise. Whether it has been well done is open to question; it has certainly been done. Ever since the Hegelian heyday philosophical writers have been variously grading the spectrum of the sciences and showing how they shade off into one another. The exercise is full of interest on its own account, and a potential source of wisdom; it should help us, by balancing the different diagrams of special knowledge, to see things whole. But it offers no direct solution to the problem of theology. However orderly our spectrum of the sciences, we cannot put theology in. Is it between the green and yellow? It is not. Beyond the infra-red or ultra-violet? No. The theologian is not picking a colour from the rainbow; he is looking at the sun.

A system of the sciences helps us to compose the picture of finite being. But all finite being is on one side, and infinite Being on the other, of the great divide. It puzzles our brains to re-assemble the image of the finite, fragmented as it is in our prismatic thought. But when we have done it, we have settled a purely domestic issue, we have tidied the furniture of our own parlour. We have done nothing yet towards bringing the Infinite into focus.

We set out to throw a bridge, and here we are bridge-breaking once more. The handsome viaduct which spans the delta of the sciences cannot be carried out across the ocean. Theology cannot be reckoned among the ways we have of viewing our environment, except by an equivocation. 'How would you like to view the picture? From the floor, or from the gallery? By what remains of daylight, or by those fluorescent tubes?'—'Thank you; I prefer to view it as the work of Tintoretto.' Viewing the picture as the work of Tintoretto may be called a way of viewing it, but not in the same sense as the previous suggestions give to 'a way of viewing'. Our several sciences and modes of knowledge are ways of getting finite reality into focus; it is quite another thing to view it as the field of a divine activity. For if you are to do that no number of mutually supplementing shots of your subjects will do; you have somehow to become aware of the divine activity exercised through them or upon them; you have (in some extended sense) to get God into focus, as well as his finite creations; and this is to go into another dimension, with which the modes of natural knowledge are not concerned.

So Theology cannot be put in the scale of science, or even of knowledge. Nevertheless, to know God is to know, and not to do anything fundamentally different; it is to accord to some real being a conscious recognition (always supposing that religious conviction has any validity whatever). And it seems we cannot say even so much as this, without implying something about the logic or the structure of the thought affirmative of God. 'To know,' or 'to acknowledge as real', when used of finites and when used of God, cannot mean two utterly different things.

What generalisation can we form wide enough to embrace the two spheres?

I propose, without any attempt at prior justification, to fix upon the inseparability of real knowledge from activity. I do not mean the mere platitude that knowledge, or (let us say) the intelligent affirmation of fact is itself an active business; the telling of a story, not its printed existence on a mental page; the painting over of a picture, not its glowing on a canvas of passive imagination. I mean nothing so innocent as this. I mean that to know real beings we must exercise our actual relation with them. No physical science without physical interference, no personal knowledge without personal intercourse; no thought about any reality about which we can do nothing but think. Is not this the highest possible generalisation of the empirical principle? Theology must be at least as empirical as this, if it is to mediate any knowledge whatever. We can know nothing of God, unless we can do something about him. So what, we must ask, can we do?

It is easy, of course, to answer 'Nothing'; an answer just as likely to be returned on pious as on impious grounds. We do anything about God? The very notion can be denounced as blasphemous. Faith begins where religious pretension ends; when we stop thinking we can do anything about God, we remove the worst obstacle to his doing something for us. Now there is certainly a place for language of this kind, but that place is the pulpit. It is a red-herring across our present line of discussion. We are not discussing whether the initiative in our salvation lies with man or with God. We are asking what man does. And our most absolute theologians know that man's salvation is not achieved by man's passivity. He may be passive to God; but his passivity to God involves and indeed is an activity on his own part. The trees were passive to Orpheus; that's why they danced. It is an old saw, that the order of knowing may reverse the order of being. According to real order, man's activity in faith proceeds from God's activity in grace. In our order of enquiry we may work back to God's activity from man's.

We are free, then, to ask what we suppose we can do about God. Before we proceed to do so, we may usefully orientate ourselves by relating our empirical principle to a familiar issue. How often we have discussed whether God's existence and his attributes can or cannot be inferred from our knowledge of the world! The question can be debated on a dozen grounds. A favourite ground to take is the topic of analogy. God's nature and way of existing, we agree, can be no more than distantly analogous to those of any created thing; and the causality by which he causes his creatures to exist can be no more than distantly analogous to any finite causality productive of a finite effect. These admissions being made, we go on to ask whether such a remoteness of analogical relation still allows the drawing of any inference from the one side to the other? If it does, we can usefully enquire into a knowledge of God derivable from knowledge of the world. If it does not, our knowledge of God must derive from an independent source; and the analogy we claim to find between the creatures and God is the sort of analogy which can be appreciated only on the basis of a prior knowledge of both terms. You could never have inferred from the painter's art the nature or the possibility of the musician's; but once acquainted with both, you can develop the analogy between them. So on this supposition, analogy or no analogy, God and the world must both in some fashion have made their print on our minds, and not the world only.

We have recalled this highly traditional topic for the sole purpose of trying our newly defined empirical principle upon it; we will do so now, taking in turn the two hypotheses just outlined. On the first hypothesis we shall be saying that the nature and existence of God are in such a sense continuous with the nature and existence of things composing the world, that we need not do anything about God himself, to have a knowledge of him. It would be with the knowledge of God as it is with the knowledge (already instanced) of planetary revolutions. Though we can do nothing about them, experiment with analogous material sufficiently discloses their nature, and the inferential extension of a physical system we can directly probe gives sufficient grounds for postulating their occurrence. In some such fashion, on the hypothesis we are considering, what we are able to do about finite beings in exploiting or exercising our relation with them is sufficient of itself for an inferential knowledge of God.

And now to take the second hypothesis, which arises from the discredit of the first. Let it be judged preposterous that any active exploitation of inter-finite relations should constitute or ground a discovery of God. Then according to our empirical principle, any knowledge we do have of him arises from some exploitation, as it were, of a relation with himself; and so there must, in the required sense, be something we can do about God.

I have put the two hypotheses as strict alternatives; but it is not necessary to discredit the first entirely, if we are to establish our need of the second. We may reason as follows. An inferential notion of deity, even if validly inferred, must be empty and schematic to the last degree. What could the most traditional argument in this line claim to prove? An Unknown, an X, qualified (I know not how) to be the supreme or maximum in a scale of active or causative beings, always supposing that such beings fall into a scale, and that the scale culminates in an absolute beyond which it is meaningless to go. So much for the divine nature. For the divine action, we harvest a crop of similar vacuities. It will be an agency which bears to the highest form of finite agency an analogy vastly more remote than that obtaining between any two finite agencies; an agency such as to stand outside the whole dimension of temporal succession or of spatial extension.

What do such definitions achieve? Even granting the postulations on which they rest, they define God neither by what he is nor by how he acts but purely by the functional position of his Being as supreme term in a speculative scale.

The vacuity of the resultant idea (if idea it can be called) is painfully evident. Never mind, we say; if an examination of the world so much as suggests such a notion to us, then the world points to God. The claim is, perhaps, overstated; but even allowing it to pass, what does it mean? Is it simply tautologous, a mere proposal to use the name 'God' for the schematic notion just described? Or is it an assertion with some substance in it, claiming for the being indicated by our notion the further characteristics of deity? If so, what are these characteristics and how do they come to be known? If they are not reached as inferences marginal to our active exploration and consequent construction of the universe, whence do they swim into our view? Must it not be from some active exploration of our relation to the First Cause himself? So the second hypothesis comes in to supplement the first.

I am well aware that I am telling a thrice-told tale, except that, with our empirical principle in mind, I am dotting the i's and crossing the t's in my own way. Pursuing the same course, we may try another of the traditional moves. We have just asked by what channel the characteristics of deity reach our knowledge; we have still to ask what anyhow they are. Now it has commonly been said that when we call the First Cause 'God' we are indeed making a significant assertion: we are saying that this causative being is solely or supremely worshipful. The remark is by no means as simple as it sounds; indeed few remarks made in philosophical discussion are. What does 'worshipful' mean? The word has an etymological history which is well-known, and which, like so many etymological histories, obscures rather than illuminates current usage. I propose to lay down the law: 'Worshipful' is taken to mean 'adorable', not as puppies and whimsies are accorded the epithet, but in the strict sense of meriting adoration. 'Adoration' is only the Latin for 'worship', after all. 'Adorable' has been debased, and 'worshippable' is a rotten word; we make do with 'worshipful'.

So the remark we quoted makes deity equivalent with 'object of worship'; it being always understood that he is not so *de facto* simply, through the accidental circumstance that people worship him; he is so *de jure*, being such as to merit adoration. Otherwise put, 'worshipful' is a typical value-word. As to value, modern theory has added little to Aristotle's definition: 'Good is what anything is after.' The philosopher meant 'the *proper* object of a *natural* appetite or aspiration.' To call anything good in the serious or intrinsic sense was to say that it had actual qualities such as to make it the proper object of pursuit; and the pursuer's so viewing it gilded those qualities with an emotive aura, the attractiveness or the prestige of being 'good'. With 'worshipful' the case is no different. A subject can be worshipful *per se* only in the sense in which a subject can be good *per se*. Nothing and no one is worshipful apart from relation to possible worshippers; yet it or he can be intrinsically worshipful, as really possessing the character which does and should attract their worship.

In Aristotle's definition, anyhow under its English dress, a blessed ambiguity attaches to the phrase 'is after'. I think, indeed, that there is the same ambivalence about the philosopher's Greek. 'What I am after' is not necessarily that of which I am in active pursuit. All heavy bodies, in Aristotle's view, were after the centre of the globe, whether they had any opportunity or none of sinking towards it. And any of us can say, 'Ah, *that's* what I'm after!' as a recognition of what he wants, before he has made the slightest move in that direction. So an object may glow with the aura of the Good, before we have stirred a step in pursuit of it, or even when conflicting desires lead us to abandon its pursuit entirely. But (if there is any truth in Aristotle's definition) nothing would be good, if the pursuit of such goods were inconceivable, to pursue them not being an open possibility. And equally it seems clear that God's worshipfulness means nothing, unless we have some stirrings towards the worshipping of him, and some sense of what to worship him would be. And so we obtain the conclusion we require: God would not be recognised as worshipful, save in relation to our worshipping. If he is so recognised, there is something we can do about God: we can worship him.

There is a romance about the unattainable; and dreamy souls may prefer birds for ever in the bush to birds in the hand. Whatever enjoyment there may be in this, it is not the enjoyment of knowledge. If we want to know how anything is good, and how good it is, we must actively pursue it, and catch it if we can; and the good that we can find in it will be proportioned to the pursuit we can make of it. To know in depth the good of a friendship we must enter into a community of action with our friend along a multiplicity of lines; this will be knowledge, whether our resultant sense of the person is or is not more thrilling than the initial impression of infinite promise, the unearthly gleam of our first encounter. Admittedly there are complications here. I may well think that there is more in every person whom God has made, than I can fathom or explore; and that the initial promisingness hints at real possibilities which our friendship fails to attain, and which, in its failure, it obscures and erases. But however much the genuine promise of good exceeds the good attained, promise is promise, it is not the good promised. And if there were no attainment, we should not even know what the promise promised us.

To return now to the worshipfulness of God. Here the disproportion between ultimate promise and proximate attainment must be infinitely greater; so that in our attitude to God an emphasis falls on the moment of wondering contemplation which in our dealings with our fellows would be inappropriate. The very use we make of the word 'worship' indicates the fact. In its wider sense it covers the whole of our activity in relation to God; in its narrower and more precise sense it means sheer adoration; and it is this narrower sense which, being the more precise, gives its general colour to the word. To worship means to adore, however much we may tell ourselves that *laborare est orare, das Denken ist auch Gottesdienst*, and so forth. A room can be swept to the worship of God, if we may so adapt George Herbert's sentiment; but sweeping rooms is not what worshipping means.

Yet however high we place the 'primacy of worship' in religious life, the philosophical point is unaffected. We adore in God a being who holds the promise of good beyond our power in this life to explore; we do not know the good by any other token than what our exploration reveals. And so it must surely be a philosophical blunder to throw a unique cognitive weight upon moments of sheer adoration, not to mention moments of sheer numinous fright. When Awfulness suddenly comes over us, we are fascinated by the promise, or if you like, the threat of we know not what. But 'we know not what' is what we do not know, and it is difficult to put so nondescript an article on the philosophical market.

In such inchoate experiences we are moved by nothing that is of theological importance, unless it is a first dawning of the thought of God; and whether it is so we shall not know until it becomes so. The thought of God—and it is our empirical principle that we can think nothing as real, about which we can do nothing but think; and to 'nothing but think' we may add the gloss 'or have emotions, either'. It is true that emotion is a rough and ready guide to practical concern, so that thoughts which stir emotion are commonly thoughts of things about which something can or must be done. Yet emotion can be misplaced to an almost indefinite extent; the doing, not the feeling, is the empirical test. Nothing can give substance to our thought of God but an experience which employs our activity in relation to God, where that activity is something other than thought itself; always allowing (as we said on a previous page) that our activity in the matter is passive towards a prior activity of God.

It may be very true, then, that in the order of the individual's experience moments of awe and of adoration may precede activity of any kind in relation to God. Yet in the order of philosophical enquiry we may usefully start with the activity, if our purpose is to see what disclosure of a divine reality takes place in religion.

Those who have wished to find in adoration an apprehension of God sufficient to itself have traditionally based themselves on the heresy of intellectual vision. Aristotle received it from Plato; he modified, but could not discard it. Reasoning towards the truth, said these philosophers, is a ladder by which we climb, but which, once we are up, we can kick down. Our thought stops working from point to point; the idea—that is to say, the truth—is self-luminous in the mind, and its being so constitutes our act of understanding it; much as the presence of a visual object in our sense of sight constitutes our act of seeing it.

Abuse of the analogy between sight and understanding is one of the great philosophical delusions. I say, abuse; it would be stupid indeed to prohibit the use. We shall go on saying 'Now I see' for 'Now I understand'. The metaphor is inevitable. As fixing in visual focus is to searching round for what we wish to see, so understanding is to wrestling with what we seek to understand. It is very proper to compare success in one medium with success in another; the propriety of the comparison is no ground for equating the media. If it were sense (which I dare say it is not) to call harmony in music what proportion is in building, it would still not follow that musical composition was a sort of architecture.

But to return to the valid analogy between understanding and sight: it goes a point further than we have specified. The eye, having picked the object out, can dwell upon it. The object may not repay the trouble; not, for example, a collar-stud under the chest of drawers; but then again it may; say a rare orchid in the tangle of grass. The mental object equally may or may not bear dwelling upon. If it does, the mind, having grasped it, can dwell upon it. Only intellectual 'dwelling upon' is no more a sort of gazing, than is the flash of intellectual perception a sort of seeing; it is just an appreciative thinking-over. One of the things that most obviously bears dwelling upon is a page of verse, since merely to master the sense is not to enjoy it at all. But it is not the sort of thing that can be enjoyed by being gazed at; it has to be run through again and again.

The best short characterisation of thinking is that it is a sort of talking to ourselves; and there are many sorts of talk, whether to ourselves or aloud. There is the talking which establishes an idea, and there is the talking which savours it. There we go, metaphor again: the metaphor of taste this time instead of sight. Never mind; every metaphor has its special use and makes its own point. Metaphors apart, we are considering the many-sidedness of language. Whenever we talk, our discourse is both guided and enriched by a whole network of association. It lies always just below the floor of consciousness. It acts in and upon the march of words, in which, and in which for the most part alone, it makes itself felt. The balance between this supporting background and the speech or thought which focusses it varies most subtly from moment to moment. When our mind is bent upon the correct formation of our mental discourse, the associative background plays its part in guiding our conscious effort by a system of invisible and as it were automatic controls; say when we are picking out an unfamiliar mental path, hammering out a new idea, developing a logical argument or interpreting an obscure set of symbols. But when we are savouring what we know already, the balance is reversed. We do not ask the patterns of association to shape our thought, once the shape is set; we let it play back upon them, and awake all the resonances of the mind; as happens when, having mastered a poem, we say it over to ourselves; when we dwell in absence on the name of a person we like; or when (alas!) we brood on a standing cause of resentment.

Such ways of employing our thought are seldom without considerable emotion; and yet we judge wrongly if we call the emotional element the sole significant addition to the plain sense of our mental speech. The enjoyment of literature is not decipherment *plus* feeling; not anyhow if 'feeling' bears its emotional sense. We may indeed say that we feel the mental resonances or background echoes of the language. But the word 'feel' in such a statement carries the metaphor of tactual sense, and not of emotion. It reminds us how we feel the stir of the air on our cheek or the textures of different jumbled silks with our hand. The point of the metaphor is, as so commonly, a point of contrast. Feels of this sort are rich, vague and un-focussed in distinction from the hard precisions of sight; and so is our sense of background depths as against our manipulation of surface units in the world of the mind.

Take the case when you say to yourself the name of the person you are fond of, placing it perhaps in some little appreciative phrase. The lines of association tingle; you have a feeling of what he is like to talk to, of the kindnesses he has done you, of any among a dozen memories about him; and at the same time you feel warmly disposed towards him—as we have just said, a quite different use of the word 'feel'. In some such manner, too, we may suppose that Aristotle, having reasoned his way to that supreme Mind which in his system moves the stars, dwelt on the idea without much discursive width or much verbal elaboration, feeling the place of such a being at the apex of existence, and at the same time feeling himself moved with admiration and desire.

When I dwell upon, or mentally contemplate, a person, my attention plays upon an object on which my bodily sight could also play. It may well be nevertheless that my mental contemplation is not concerned with what my eye could see; not with my friend's look, but with his conduct. What summarises or focusses itself in my repetition of his name may be a story, not a picture. The story itself, if I were to expand it in detail, need not, and probably would not, be set out in pictorial images. It might be conceived in the more basic terms of personal action; what my friend did and meant, in interaction with what I did and meant. It is true that the interplay of personal action involves the mediation of eyesight, except where the parties are blind, and of hearing, unless they are deaf. But the story may still be a story of what they mutually and responsively did, not a story of how anything sounded or how anything looked.

Perhaps we have rambled too far in the general description of mental contemplation. Let us come without more ado to the point which concerns us. The mental act of contemplating God may evoke imaginary pictures; in thinking of the divine fatherhood I may recall the radiant benignity of my father's face, as I can well remember it. But even in using such pictures of God, I am aware of their purely conventional value. They stand for something else, say the active benevolence or fostering care of a

Creator. And so far as my poor gift for contemplating goes, I may dwell upon God in this aspect without any picture or shadow of a picture, my 'idea' being the summary or the focussing of a story. The lovingkindness I contemplate is God's calling us into existence, his stamping us with the likeness of his Godhead, his redemption of us by the incarnation of his Son, his offering us the gifts of his grace, his forgiveness of our back-slidings, his renewal of our titles to his favour: the catalogue, so absurd to unbelievers and so sacred to believers, sounds out of place in a philosophical context. But however that may be, these are the divine histories which echo to the naming of divine mercy.

The conclusion we draw is that the contemplation of God is dependent upon the experience of his action, however that experience is obtained. But I can see my mystically-minded readers full of protest. 'Your conclusion only follows' they declare, 'because you have ignored true contemplation entirely. Contemplation, indeed! You have discussed nothing more advanced than meditation. In actual contemplation the soul is not engaged in gathering the fragrance of old histories; she undergoes the present Act of God.'

What shall we say to this accusation? We admit the fact. The sense we have given to contemplation though venerable, is not mystical. In old philosophy contemplation, *theoria*, was the counting over of intellectual treasures, the austere appreciation of principles, the sheer realisation of thoughts. We took our start from the antique notion, and merely gave a modern account of it. We also extended its range to less daunting fields: from theorems to poems, from ultimate ends to loving friends. But the meaning of the word undergoes an altogether more abrupt alteration if we follow it down into mystical theology. In the language of that heavenly science, the name of contemplation is denied to those ruminative exercises we have mentioned, and restricted to an ecstatic passivity, in which ideas, if present, are encumbrances, and in which the divine Act seizes the will.

The history of words is beset by a thousand accidents, and rationalised summaries of their mutations awake the worst suspicions of the learned. Let us hope it is not more misleading than such statements inevitably are to say that what happened to the word 'contemplation' was this: mystical minds, in using the term, had their attention fixed upon what is immediate in an intellectual touch upon God; and when their experience taught them that what is immediate is not intellectual, they still continued to speak of 'contemplation'. If this is anything like a true history, the mystical usage of the word only goes to support our case. The idea of God summarises the history of his action; the soul's direct touch upon God is not through any (self-luminous) idea of him.

What distinguishes mystical 'contemplation' is not its content but its dynamic. Instead of exercising his will in devout attention to God, the 'contemplative' feels his will to be exercised in him by God; and at the point where this happens, distinct intelligible content vanishes. And why? Because the man is no longer telling himself anything. Nevertheless the conviction must be haunting the penumbra of consciousness, that the overpowering visitant of the soul is God; for otherwise the experience loses all spiritual importance. So far as the mere pathology of the state is concerned, there is no need for any visitant to be supposed, whether demonic or divine; the subject may take his condition to be mere abnormality, a temporary disease of consciousness. The religious value of the ecstasy lies in its disclosing itself as a divine effect; the significance of the disclosure is dependent on a prior knowledge of God; and this knowledge, in turn, will summarise much narrative about the actions of God. Nor can the actions of God summarised in the prior idea of God be God's seizures of mystical minds; for any number of such seizures, by themselves, would be meaningless. The mystic's conviction is not, that the Seizer of the will seizes the will; it is that God seizes the will.

Shall we be so bold as to go a step further, and assign mystical 'contemplation' a place in the balance of spiritual life? We may begin by saying that dwelling upon the thought of God is obviously more like dwelling upon a friend than upon a poem. The poem is the very formula we recite: that is the unalterable core of it, whatever may be its changing resonances. But the friend is a living person, and though our knowledge of him is entirely based on his past history and ours, it is taken by us as information bearing upon the present and the future. As to the present, we are happy to think of the man we like as actually existent; as to the future, we look forward to further exchanges with the man we have come to know. So the idea we have of a friend is ambiguously related to the friend himself. It is directed upon his present and his future, but it is based on his past—for even if we think he has changed or will change, our grounds for thinking so must lie in our past experience of him; we have no other.

And now to consider our thoughts of God. God has not a past, present and future, nor will he change. But our evidence of his action, whatever it may be, lies in our past. He will not change, as our neighbour may change. But then neither is he limited to a fixed nature or formed character as our neighbour is. He is the creator, the infinite source of innovation; his fresh actions will not belie his former promises, but his new ways of showing himself faithful to his old purposes will endlessly surprise us. And so the believer who approaches a present and living God has a motive for breaking the moulds of his thought and banishing all he knows of God: let him put no obstacles in the way of God's being and doing what he chooses to be or to do there and then in the believer's soul. We have said that in contemplating the thought of a friend we may rejoice in his present existence, but that for contact with him we must look towards future opportunities. When we contemplate God, the case is not the same. We do indeed see our future as in his hands, but he will never in this life be more immediate to us than he is now: the very act by which we attend to him may be the act by which he works in us; the mystic clears his mind of lumber and dares to hope he may be occupied by the God with whom he is occupied.

34

It is with reluctance that I, least mystical of men, reflect upon a subject in which I am so little qualified. The last thing I want to pretend is to fathom the mystical fact. It is enough for our present purposes if we can assign it some sort of place in relation to our knowledge of God, and to God's self-revealing activity. Our thesis is that our thought of God is the summary of a tale which narrates the actions of God; and it can do no harm to such a thesis to acknowledge moments which, setting the thought of God aside, make room for his action's living touch.

CHAPTER III

SPIRITUAL SCIENCE

WE set out in the last chapter to look for a proper starting-point, and we hit upon the empirical principle 'We can think about nothing—that is, about no (supposed) reality—about which we can do nothing but think'. We concluded that the disclosure of God must lie in the exercise of a relation with God. Approaching the matter from another angle, we have since been seeing that to think about God is in any case to think about his activity; and it is with his activity that our activity must be presumed to engage. It is the conviction of orthodox religion that his activity is primary, and ours very secondary, in any interchange. But in the order of philosophical enquiry it seems better to start with our activity, since if there is one thing we can be presumed to know, it is what we ourselves do. What God may be said to do is another matter; that is the mystery. We will proceed, therefore, from the better known to the less known, from our action to God's.

Our question is, 'What can we do in relation to God?' We have already seen that 'We can worship him' offers no answer. For if 'worship' is taken in the narrow or specific sense, it refers precisely to that adoring contemplation which is nothing but a dwelling on the thought of God, and which presupposes a knowledge of his action. Whereas, if 'worship' is taken in an extended sense, it refers in general to whatever we can do in honour of God, and fails to specify what that might be.

One way to answer the question, 'What can we do?' would be to launch into an enumeration of pious acts and attitudes. But should not we lose our way in an infinity of detail? We are lucky to have extricated ourselves from the mystical thicket;

let us not, for heaven's sake, plunge headlong into a pastoral and ascetical forest. We want to approach the religious facts with a clear notion of what we are looking for. We do not simply want to know what things we can do in relation to God, but in how many significantly different ways we can engage our activity with his.

To reformulate the question thus is to imply some notion of mutually engaged activity, or (for short) of interaction, applicable to the case of man and God and merely requiring more exact definition by the addition of specific marks. But have we any such notion? We can think if we like that when we have reached a special definition of interaction with divine agency we shall be in a position to form a generalisation covering all types of interaction, interaction with the divine included. But it seems fairly obvious that we have no such generalisation ready-made beforehand.

A simple comparison may illustrate the point. Let us suppose that we accept the evidence for the mysterious Yeti of the Himalayas. We shall probably assume that it is an otherwise unknown species of land-mammal. We know what the general description of land-mammals is, and we have no reason to imagine that the special characteristics of the Yeti, when and if discovered, will call for a revision of the generic idea. But it is possible to take another supposition, and it is this that is relevant to our argument. Let the evidence force us to the conclusion that though it leaves mammal-like traces, the creature cannot be a mammal, still less a reptile or a bird. If that is so, we simply do not know what sort of creature it is, nor how our concept of living animal may need stretching to cover the case; not, that is, until by subtle reasoning on by happy discovery we settle to our satisfaction the nature of this unique being. Only then can we hope to construct a generalisation which will cover it and other known biological kinds under one umbrella of definition. But that is to anticipate; while the discovery is still to be made, how do we guide our researches, or guess what to look for? Having no exact idea to go upon, we are bound to use a model which we hope may be proximate, though we are convinced it is not exact. We shall presumably look for signs of a mammal-like creature, while holding ourselves in readiness to drop mammalian requirements on this side or on that as the evidence may force us to do. Apart from the use of a supposedly proximate model, we could scarcely conduct a research of any kind. We could do little more than stand dazedly about, waiting for evidence to jump up and hit us on the head.

Human interaction with the divine is not (to believers) so problematic an object as the Yeti, for it is something which they take to be embedded in their actual practice of religion. But it is something which they have not isolated, focussed or defined; they are not able in advance of philosophical enquiry to say what sort of interaction it is; and so it seems that they are bound to approach the enquiry with what they hope is a proximate model in mind. There are several sorts of interaction known to us; which do we use as a guide in approaching the theological case?

Is not the first and most obvious thing to say 'Personal interaction, not physical'? The inapplicability of the model offered by physical method seems scarcely to need demonstration. By systematic physical interference we obtain knowledge of the habitual action of natural agents, a habitual action grounded in their determinate constitutions; it is only in so far as their constitutions are determinate and their action consequently uniform, that we can discover anything about them by the physical method. Unless God is a finite determinate force, bound by natural law, he cannot be known in this sort of way. Experience of the physical type can never tell us anything about him, except that he has tied finite energies in the patterns he has assigned them. Indeed, it cannot tell us so much; we should have to know already that God was the prime creative cause, before we could say that the course found to be taken by natural process was a course on which God had set it.

There seems no more to be said—'Ah, but there is, and plenty', breaks in an indignant voice. 'You make short work of the physical model, by assuming that it would have to fit the divine case exactly. But that's contrary to your own proposal—the model can be no more than proximate at best. The Yeti of your parable was not to be defined as a mammal; the mammalian model was to be a rough-and-ready guide, and we were not to throw it over at the first brush with conflicting evidence; we were to be prepared to adapt it as the facts might seem to require. Of course experiment with nature yields natural knowledge; but what about experiment with spirit? Are there no reliable uniformities to be discovered in the spiritual realm? It is the best part of a hundred years now since someone wrote a bestseller called 'Natural Law in the Spiritual World'; yet the line of investigation so suggested is still waiting to be properly taken up. Vested interests in mythology have proved too powerful. When shall we substitute a scientific for a mythical account of the spiritual forces on which religion has always known how to draw?'

What shall we say to this protest? We shall of course point out that the use made of the contrasting terms 'scientific' and 'mythical' is a rank appeal to prejudice. The most scientific account is not the most naturalistic account, but the most accurate, on whichever side accuracy lies. If the truth of the case requires something like personal categories to express it, no light is shed on the issue by calling personal language mythical. But all this is mere skirmishing. We must go to the heart of the matter if the debate is ever to be worthwhile. So let us invite our spiritual scientist to tell us something about these spiritual forces on which religious life has always drawn. If his case is to mean anything, they must be energies or principles of some kind which operate so regularly, that systematic experience on our part can lead to an acquaintance with their ways.

Our spiritual scientist will agree so far; only he will be anxious to forestall unfair criticism. 'You are going to tell me' he says, 'that a reliable science of the spiritual does not in fact exist. How should it, when the territory is all bedevilled with superstition? The scientific method has only begun to take over the spiritual realm. Give us a chance. However far we go I dare say that we shall not obtain in the spiritual sphere anything like the accuracy of physical law. It is easy to guess good reasons why so perfect a result should be unattainable. But then it is no part of my case that anything of the sort is to be hoped for, let alone that it has been achieved. If you ask me to what available evidence I appeal, I can tell you simply enough. I appeal to the broad fact that spiritual practices are so far fruitful that spiritual religion has been able to survive. It is possible to recommend religious exercises, customs and attitudes with some confidence that they will attract the action of what theologians call "Grace". If they fail to do so, we look for obstacles and we remove them; or perhaps we adapt our precepts more carefully to the character and circumstances of the person. I am very willing to grant that spiritual practice, like medical practice, is an art, rather than a science. Nevertheless, the art of medicine presupposes the science of physiology; and if there is an art of spiritual practice, there must surely be laws of spiritual being, whether we can define them approximately or not.'

In the speech we have composed for him, the spiritual scientist has made two points. The first is that his case does not stand or fall with the achievement of high accuracy in spiritual science; and this point we are happy to concede. His other point is, that the effective value of spiritual precepts is evidence for his thesis; and this we deny. The evidence he offers on this head makes neither for him nor for us. To say that God deals personally with us is not to say that he acts by caprice. The dependability of grace may result from the ordinance of a sovereign will, just as well as from the constant nature of a force. Since no argument lies in either direction we do not wish to take the question up on this sort of ground. We would wish rather to press for information, as to what the spiritual force is supposed to be.

'What is it supposed to be?' our friend replies. 'The question is out of order, surely. We are engaged in an approach to an unknown, or at least an undefined, with the object of discovering what it is. You cannot tell me that my method of investigation is unjustified, because I do not know the answer to the question

I am setting out to solve. If I knew the answer, I should not propose a method for solving it.'

No, you would not, we must concede in reply, but neither could you propose a method of enquiry after something not even provisionally conceived. This predicament is very general. We cannot look for anything, unless we have some notion what we are looking for, but that doesn't mean that we have no need to look, or that discovery will teach us nothing beyond what we know already. We are at present asking ourselves what model will be most appropriate to guide our examination of the mysterious interaction between the human and the divine. How can we possibly choose, if we have no notion at all of the reality to which the model is to apply? If we cannot see how the physical model can be transferred to the case, without involving a description of the divine reality which strikes us as preposterous, then we shall prefer some other model to the physical. Physical method can undergo great modifications, as it does in several well-established sciences; but there are limits to any conceivable modification which would allow it still to be itself. If there is no uniformly-acting agent of a determinate constitution for us to interact with, the physical model simply does not apply. Merely to say that the agent is spiritual, not physical, is to take refuge in a cloud of mystery. I do not know what 'spiritual' means unless it denotes the higher functions of personal activity. Surely the spiritual scientist does not suppose himself to be in contact with a bodiless person, exercising none but the higher functions of mind or will, and yet acting upon him after the manner of a natural force, and not as one person on another?

'Look' says our spiritual scientist, 'you are adopting the tone of ridicule, and two can play at that game. But I will not retort. Please let us keep on a philosophical level. You are talking as though (theology apart) there were two exclusive alternatives: natural relation to a natural force, or personal relation to a person. A moment's reflection will convince you that it isn't so. There is a third possibility, natural relation to a person. Let me explain what I mean. By personal relation I mean the relation which is exemplified in dialogue. My words or my conduct express my intention towards you and you respond in conduct or in words expressing your intention towards me. Your action occasions mine, but only through meaning and through choice. With this we contrast natural relation, where the effect is occasioned on principles of causal uniformity.—Now there is one sort of natural relation with persons which is evident but uninteresting. You, by personal action, can cause physical effects on my body. For example, when you talk to me, my response may go by meaning and choice, but my hearing of your voice goes by physical rules. There is, however, a more interesting case than this; when action on your part conditions my voluntary responses themselves without my knowing what you are at, or even seeing your hand in the business at all. We resent being played upon without our consent or knowledge, and so we are inclined to pick on sinister examples, such as subliminal advertising, or perhaps some of the brain-washing tricks. But creditable cases are just as common, as when we put a child into a good temper by indirect means. Something very much like this relation obtains between different strands of activity within a single personality: the fully conscious action with which I identify myself is conditioned by a mass of intentions and policies on which I have acted and shall act, but which are not present at the moment to my mind. The conditioning must surely go by general rules, and the success (such as it is) of psychological science goes to show that it does. So you see that there is plenty of analogy for a natural relation between personal action and a personal activity conditioning it. And since God's being and action are on any showing vastly more mysterious to us than those of our fellow-beings or even those at the back of our own mind, it is reasonable enough that he should condition us in ways we do not understand. We could then have some quasi-scientific grasp of the relation of conditionedness, and some art or technique of putting ourselves in the way of it, or of opening ourselves to it.'

We must be impervious to shame if we do not feel rebuked by

this speech. There is evidently nothing absurd about the spiritual scientist's conception, and there is much in what he says with which we are bound to agree. The action of God is highly mysterious on any showing; the most sanguine of us must be largely content to hope that divine Grace may support and condition our wills in ways of which we are unaware; and in thinking of this support we shall very naturally use a mixture of analogy drawn partly from the way our neighbours may condition us and partly from the way in which we are conditioned by our own subconscious mind. All this we are happy to admit. But we are still mystified about the relation of such suppositions to the empirical principle. If they were offered as metaphysical hypothesis they might stand, but we are being asked to consider them in an empirical context. So we are bound to enquire why we should believe in the hidden action of Grace. Compare the two models by way of analogy. How do I know that my neighbours purposely condition my action? Why, I have the recipe; I do it to them; and they confess from time to time that they have done it to me. How do I know that there are buried strands of purpose in my own mind, conditioning my explicit choice? For the simple reason that these strands of purpose are mine; at other times I consciously develop them; I can revive them by way of memory now, and perceive their bearing on my immediate conduct.

In both these types of case we have a way round behind the scenes which admits us to a knowledge of the secret. What is there to resemble this in the experience of Grace? Our spiritual scientist's appeal is to the availability of gracious forces (it would be safer to say, gracious effects) on condition of the following of spiritual precepts. A very proper appeal for an empiricist to make. Only how far will it carry us? Why should not the gracious forces be lodged in our own being, and in whatever external conditions are adapted to it, or foster it? On what grounds, anyhow, is the spiritual scientist to decide that they are not? It is no news that there are sources of available energy and of positive desire corked down in the cellars of the human psyche or evocable from environmental values; it is no news that certain employments of thought, certain cultivations of attitude, certain policies of choice are better than others for conjuring them up. Stripped of their mythological trappings, why should not the spiritual precepts come down to practical directions for getting the best out of ourselves and the best out of our environment? On an empirical view, it is the most economical hypothesis, surely.

'You have certainly hit on a crucial point this time' our spiritual scientist replies. 'If you had wanted to drive a wedge into the empiricist ranks, you could scarcely have picked a more divisive topic. To change the metaphor, you have thrown us a tempting bait; I refuse it; but some of my friends will swallow it, hook, line and sinker. They will agree that religion is nothing but saintly life, and that its precepts are techniques for ranging your whole self behind such a programme of living. And if some of us gently point out to them that the precepts are largely concerned with worship of the divine, our friends reply that they can't help it; it just is so that in the present phase of human culture spiritual exercises gain added support from our telling ourselves pretty tales, and addressing ourselves to fictitious beings. The use of mythical personification is not very surprising, if one considers that we use such personifications in entering into colloquy with detached functions of our own mind; and if mythology is to be tolerated at all, the build-up of my very best self into a sovereign demanding unqualified reverence is not inappropriate. Abstractly considered, there are many higher authorities. But for me, in the moment of decision, there is none: the law of this god is my absolute.

'I have been reporting to you' (continues our spiritual scientist) 'what our out-and-outers say. Others of us feel unable to go so far. We cannot write off the otherness, the transcendence, of the object of our worship so easily. It appears to us that our extremists are falsifying the religious phenomenon. An attitude of devotion is the heart of religion and devotion cannot be offered to oneself. No doubt our own best thought demands our limitless loyalty, but that is loyalty by metaphor. The genuine article is the loyalty we owe our best friend, and our loyalty to God is more like this. We have been saying all along that the life of religion is an interaction. It is an interaction with some mysterious other, not with ourselves.'

· My dear man, we reply to our kind interlocutor, I find my heart warming towards you. I hope you will not mind my saying that the cleavage in your party-ranks which you confess is even deeper than you admit. Your left-wingers emerge as sentimental atheists—sentimental, I allow, but atheists all the same; whereas you are one of us, a good agnostic theist. Agnostic, certainly, but aren't we all? I have yet to meet the Christian philosopher who claimed to have comprehended God.

'Thank you for your good opinion' he says, 'and I can assure you it would give me nothing but pleasure to clasp the proffered hand. Only I should be sorry to win your good graces under false pretence, and I doubt if I can honestly bracket myself with you as a theist. I part company with our extremists by upholding the otherness of the divine, but I associate myself with their distrust of mythic images. I attended a conference of your friends lately and found myself deeply embarrassed by the language in which the discussion proceeded. I can romp happily with the extremists of our party through an orgy of shared iconoclasm.'

I don't doubt it, dear sir, we reply; but then it is an old observation that a common dislike is the easiest ground of agreement. We all hate tyranny, but when shall we agree on our receipes for exercising freedom? It is when we come to advance positive propositions that we discover our divergences; and it still seems to me that in your fundamental assertions you and your extremer friends are poles apart. The difference, I think, will soon emerge if you will allow me to press you a little further on the otherness of the divine.

You disagree with your friends when they identify the divine with the highest or the deepest (which is it?) in themselves. But I do not suppose you want to find the God of Grace elsewhere than in the soul. How shall I express the difference between you, then? I see it in a picture, and I will expose it in all its crudity. Life-in-grace is a plant. According to your friends, the whole growth from root to fruit is contained in their own being; the root may be underground, but it's they, none the less. You draw the line in another place. The human part of the growth is no more than a branch. The stock and root of grace are outside the confines of the created being.

I state the difference in a stupid figure because I do not know how else to state it; and I should particularly value your help towards casting it into a less questionable shape. I must say that I get scant assistance from the theologians who are fellow-travellers with you. They tell me to think of the divine as 'the ground of my being' or even as being or existence in general. Such expressions leave me in a perfect fog. I could attach meaning to them only as part and parcel of metaphysical systems long discredited. It is perhaps no wonder that theological modernists, feeling for words, come up with bits of Plato or of Hegel. The past dies hard; according to C. G. Jung, his patients dream mediaeval alchemy. Dead systems may supply living metaphors. Only it does not consort with the empirical approach to be content with them.

Will you help me to pinpoint the difference between your extremer allies and yourself in more empirical terms? I can see that it can be stated emotionally; feelings of awe and self-abasement seem appropriate in face of a mysterious Other, which would be incongruous accompaniments of the most earnest-minded self respect. But an emotional difference is surely inadequate to the case. Emotion may point the way to appropriate action; but it is our action, not our emotion, which establishes the nature of what we are up against. And so far as action is concerned, will not you and your friends be doing the same thing? Each party will be using techniques of meditation, recollection and so forth, to draw on available grace. So what's the odds? What is the cash-value of the difference between you?

'You have pickled a rod for my back' says our interlocutor, 'but before I bend over and take a beating I should like to know why mine is any more vulnerable than yours. You ask me how I justify an insistence on the otherness of God, when all I can do is draw upon a grace which my atheistic allies locate in their own being. I pass the question back to you. What can you do but draw on the same grace by similar exercises? So how do you justify your insistence on the otherness of God?'

The question is put to us, and if we find a certain embarrassment in answering, it is not because the answer is difficult to find, it is because it sounds so arrogant. We are challenged to explain how the doctrine we profess liberates a fuller or more genuine life-in-grace than that professed by some of the most high-minded and virtuous people alive, the religious atheists. To shift the odium would require a long apology, which may, I hope, be taken as read. Say if you will that we credit these people with a theism of the heart which their mouths in vain belie; say that God rewards eminent sincerity with uncovenanted blessings. Say anything you like that may serve to defend our modesty; only let us get on with the argument.

We are perfectly clear that for us there is a positive and practical value in asserting the otherness of God. For it means that we exercise our relation with him as a personal relation. God is not, indeed, out there in space beside us, like one of our neighbours; he is at the causal root of our being, and of every being; and it is through our root (to maintain the metaphor) that we receive his Grace. But his otherness for us lies in this, that his life is personal to him, it is not ours; that he has a will after which we enquire, a judgment to which we submit, a forgiveness we implore, a succour we seek; that the personal character of our relation with him is the very form of it, not a metaphorical trapping which can be thought away while any substance remains.

To take this position amounts to saying that the personal model, not the physical, is the only model for our interaction with God which can direct our approach to the heart of the

47

matter. The physical model reveals its inadequacy by blotting out the very subject we come to study, the divine. For we challenge anyone to tell us what middle position is tenable between a serious personalism in religion, and that pious atheism which has no other god than the backside of human nature.

The use of the physical model appears at first sight to accord well with the empirical spirit; but if it leads to the postulation of a divine Other that is anything but frankly personal in nature it leads to a supposition strangely out of place in an empirical system. A speculative system, founded on a contentious interpretation of the order of being, or totality of the world, might arrive at so artificial a concept as that of a non-personal Absolute; and having done so, might make shift to square philosophical dogma with religious life. Let the God of faith be the image of the Absolute, so mythologised as to be made *sensible au coeur*. If, on the other hand, we start from the God *sensible au coeur* and make a direct interpretation of the faith-interaction, what sense can there be in postulating a transcendent Other that is anything but person? What empirical relevance can it have?

'I will venture to take you up on that point' says the friend with whom we have been disputing all along. 'The motive for rejecting the dogma of divine personality may be as practical as it well could be. The imposition of the personal image on the God to whom one prays, so far from liberating the life of Grace, may be utterly inhibiting to it. Confine the divine nature and action within the lineaments of a personality with whom you are (so to speak) in converse, and the converse is stifled. The way out is well-known. One says to God, "You are not this, you are not as I. I know not what you are. Be what you will; shine on me as light, feed me as bread, be the air of my breathing, be the energy of my act, be the love in my heart." The personal is an image under which we must often view God; it is not he.'

I know, we reply; the experience is common. Only the conclusion to be drawn from it needs careful thought. I hope you will not feel that I am letting down the level of the discussion if I take a fairy-tale example. Menelaus has caught Proteus. He says to him, 'Be what you like, I will not let you go: be fire, be water, fish or lion, or be the Old Man of the Sea.' It is surely implied in such an address that Proteus is more essentially the Old Man of the Sea than he is any other of his manifestations; for only a person, a man with a magical overplus, can be credited with the choice of appearing at will in any one of half-a-dozen guises. It does not belong to fire or water to exercise such options.

But we must try a more philosophical approach to the matter. Consider the phrase 'interpreting God by the personal image.' The phrase can mean either of two things, which, psychologically at least, are vastly different. It can mean simply that the person-category gives shape to your thinking about God, or your intercourse with him, whether you attend to the fact or not. Or again it can mean that you consciously apply the image to God; you draw (let us say) such inferences about him from personal situations as are virtually drawn in several of the Gospel parables. The nature and the importance of the distinction can be readily grasped if we apply it to the analogous case of knowing one's neighbours. Consider the phrase 'My own personality is my clue to the understanding of my fellow-man.' In one sense this is undeniably and universally true. To understand my neighbour as what he is, a person, is to realise that he is (so to speak) inside himself as I am inside myself; that he is on the issuing, not the receiving end of his personal activities; that for him to act or to experience over a whole gamut of possible experiences and acts is what it would be for me so to act or to experience. Were I not consciously myself, I should have no clue to his being himself.

But for the most part the clue of self-knowledge acts automatically in our experience of others. It provides the form of our thought, it does not enter into the matter of our thinking. On certain occasions, but they are comparatively rare, being at a loss to see what our neighbour is at, we do what we call 'putting ourselves in his place'. The manoeuvre is a poor second-best. In the ordinary way we allow our interpretation of him to be directly controlled by his audible words on his visible deeds. It is with conduct as it is with speech; I should not understand you if I were not a mind like you, and similarly furnished to a great extent. But being so equipped, I take your meaning straight; it is an unhappy moment when I have to go through the motions of asking myself what I should mean by such words, were I in your place, and were I to utter them.

It would be too much to claim that in the understanding of our neighbours self-knowledge provides a pure category, the human-as-such, imposing neither limit nor distortion on our understanding of any individual man. My knowledge of mankind is narrowed and coloured on every side by what I individually am. My selfhood is a limit, certainly; yet it is a limit which is highly elastic. I never escape from it (how could I?) but I let it be stretched as far as it will go by the otherness of my neighbour's conduct. I do not commonly confine my idea of him in the straitjacket of self-knowledge, as I do on those unlucky occasions when I 'put myself in his place'.

When we turn from knowledge of our neighbour to knowledge of God, the distinction we have been drawing becomes all the sharper. On the one side, we have far stronger reasons than we have in the case of our neighbour to work a direct and conscious analogy from ourselves to God; for (to put it mildly) the phenomena of divine speech addressed to our ears and of divine intervention in our lives are less plentiful, or should we say, less intelligible, than the phenomena of neighbourly intervention and neighbourly speech. And so we have every motive to supplement any such direct experience with parabolic inference.

But then on the other side we have far stronger reasons in religion than in neighbourly intercourse for avoiding a conscious analogic inference which imposes our own form of being and action on the other. My neighbour is at least a man; I may blur his individuality, I shall not falsify his species, by interposing my own image between my mental eye and him. Whereas God is not a man, except by his act of condescension in the saving incarnation. True, the very possibility of intercourse between man and God supposes the dogma of our creation in his likeness, at whatever remove; it does not justify us in limiting him to our littleness. So we have every motive to avoid direct parabolic analogy, any limiting interposition of the personal image between our eyes and God; for the only personal image we can put forward will be the human image. We shall need so to loosen our thought, so to banish our prejudices, that the divine action may be free to manifest itself in us under any image, or through any fact, which may act as a vehicle of it.

We have laid down opposite necessities—for the use of human parable and for the avoidance of it. How can the two necessities be met? Not both at once, surely. Our thought oscillates between two poles, the negation of the image, and its parabolic use. If the hesitation of the empirically-minded to affirm the personality of God is a defence of their liberty to make the negative move, we have no quarrel with them. The personal image is indeed an ambivalent symbol in religious thinking; but the basic personal category remains inescapable, so long as God is a real Other to us.

Before we close the chapter, there is a loose end which requires tying in. Our spiritual scientist proposed that the model for divine action upon the creature might be found in the natural action of personal forces, as when the mere cheerfulness of a companion radiates good-humour. We protested that if the being or virtue of God gave us none but such 'natural' support, we should never have either the motive or the ground for affirming God. But once we have that affirmation as the function of an interaction with God's will, we are free to make whatever supplementary use of the 'natural' model we judge to be sound. On the side of piety, we may think it proper to acknowledge a general radiation of divine influence alongside a particular operation of divine purpose; on the side of speculation we may suppose that the method by which divine purpose itself moves or guides us is something like a varied and voluntarily directed influence. I do not for the present wish to attach positive value to such ideas; I simply desire to acknowledge that nothing has been said in the preceding argument to discredit them.

CHAPTER IV

GRACE AND FREEWILL

IF we philosophise about physical enquiry, nobody blames us for concentrating on the most advanced physical work of our time, and extracting our philosophical logic from that. We are not accused of narrowmindedness because our theory of scientific procedure condemns the alchemists' method or picks a hole in Sir Isaac Newton. The most serious philosophising is an examination of what we seriously think, and we are not, or should not be, Newtonians.

It is the same if we philosophise on morals or aesthetics. We are concerned with the general forms of moral or aesthetic thinking, not with the defence of particular judgments, whether aesthetic or moral. Yet it would be odd if our formal theory did not so far square with our own serious judgments, as to make them perfect instances of the form we lay down. Nobody blames us because our theory of aesthetics fails to accommodate a taste which identified visual beauty with type-perfection (the pin-up woman, the dog-fancier's greyhound, the copybook geranium). Not that we are justified in simply canonising our own judgments. We may fairly be called upon to show particular reason for preferring our judgments to rival estimates; indeed one of the philosopher's concerns will be to exhibit the logic of such polemical reasoning.

Or again, if we philosophise about religion. Our business is not to justify particular beliefs or practices; and yet we should not be behaving like serious men if our theory were such that our most vital convictions or most earnest practices would not serve to illustrate it. Here also we are denied the right to stand on simple prejudice; our very philosophy must show the nature of the argument we conduct against forms of religion judged by us inferior, and equally the nature of the persuasion which wins us to adopt the positions of others. Only we cannot do every sort of thinking at once. There is a day for discussing rival religions, and there is a day for considering the logic of what we seriously take religion to be. Let today be a day of the latter kind. We propose to pick up the personal model which our last chapter commended, and apply it to religion as we know it. And so all questions of the form 'But do not the Buddhists . . .?' are ruled out of court. Not that they are unimportant questions; they are extremely important. Only they belong to another occasion.

The object of religion is to establish a positive relation between men and their Creator; and so, if we are to use the personal model, we may take it up in the special form of a happy relationship between friends. For the purpose of the application we are to make, we wish to isolate two factors in any such relationship. First, there is the complex of activities, whatever they may be, pursued by either party. Second, there is the satisfactory relation maintained between the two personal activity-complexes, a relation wherein the friendship may be said to lie. This relation must be itself lively and must enliven the activities it relates; it must join them also in some sort of pattern. If we ask 'What sort of pattern?' different friendships will yield us different answers. You might think that every friendship unites the parties in common pursuits or in harmony of interests. But it is not so. The variety of friendship finds a fair and revealing example in the protean character of friendly conversation. The subjects of interest to the conversationalists, and the views they take on those subjects, may widely diverge; only they must be concerned with one another's opinions and ready to sympathise with each other's interests; they must enter into one another's minds and they must lay bare their own. Perhaps, indeed, no friendship worthy of the name comes down to an endless sparring-match and nothing more. Friends must find common ground on which to meet, and lines along which with good conscience they can further one another's hopes; but we cannot determine *a priori* where that ground will lie, or which way those lines will run.

Friends make promises to one another, implicit or explicit, and if they are honest men, do not break them, except for the sort of reasons which everywhere absolve the fulfilment of undertakings. But outside the field of common reliability, a friend's response to his friend's advance is not determinate. We can only know that it will be friendly, and that it will be truly his. A and B are friends, A stands for Parliament and B is of the other party. It is not evident that friendship obliges B to canvass for a dear man against a cherished principle; nor is it evident that the friendship will suffer if he refuses.

Friendship is a thing made up as it goes along. By actions directed at our friends we draw responses from them and shape our further action by reference to what they do; and in the process of such free mutuality we come to know the men with whom we deal. In the strict sense of the word 'empirical', acquaintance with friends is a more empirical business, more of a perpetual try-on, than acquaintance with physical energies. In the physical realm we deliver ourselves from a constant improvisation by forming the perfect generalisation. In our experience of persons we use no such guide; no hypothesis falls with a crash to the ground if our neighbours act counter to our makeshift inductions. Our friend will not, of course, do just anything; the response he makes will be such as to be humanly and morally possible; and after the event we may fairly hope to integrate it with our total picture of the person. But that is another thing entirely.

The absence of flat predictability from our friends' responses does not entail that there can be no art of friendship, no precepts on which I can rely to further it. I can know that I should think of a friend positively and warmly, and take trouble to appreciate what he is at; should study his happiness, should curb any egotism on my part likely to obstruct our intercourse. Precepts of this kind have a general validity through the relation they bear to constant facts. And what are these facts? They are the nature of friendly relationship as such, and the psychology of my own affections. They are independent of the special pursuits, decisions and actions of this friend or that. I can add by-laws to my art of friendship in view of my friend's idiosyncrasies, and modify them as he, or my picture of him, develops. The general rules of the art stand on another foundation and remain unaffected.

It is time that we turned to the application of our analogy. The due relation between a man and his Creator establishes a positive rapport between activity on both sides—involving (ideally speaking) the whole of the man's activity, and such part of the divine as concerns him. At first sight the relation seems unlike friendship in being utterly one-sided; the man's activity is to be brought into total conformity with God's, and there is no reciprocity. But this one-sidedness is compensated by an equal one-sidedness the other way. That part of the divine activity which concerns us is devoted to our self-realisation, not to God's. (Also, of course, to the development of our fellow-creatures, but that's another point.)

It seems vain to pretend that any advances towards God on our part command any particular guaranteed response on his. In the last chapter we heard a good deal from our spiritual scientist about the general dependableness of spiritual precepts. But it seems proper to compare these with the general art of friendship of which we were speaking just now. The validity of the precepts has a double basis; human psychology and the intrinsic nature of relation to one's Creator. There are ways of thinking about the action and will of God, *whatever he may be pleased to do*, which tend to keep us in friendship with his will.

Admittedly there is a complication here. To found the force of the precepts in our own nature is not to place the ground of them outside the action of God; for in the view of religion (which we are exploring here) nature is a divine ordinance, and all natural effects, so far as they tend to a positive end, are the handiwork of God. Nevertheless, a man devoting himself to his Creator must set himself on his own side of the relationship and regard as 'I' what goes to make his action a going concern; 'I' must include the nature of my mind, whatever it excludes. The man is bound to trust God for letting him go on being himself, while he engages himself with God's will; and to take on trust as his whatever belongs to his being himself.

The workings of the human psyche are only loosely uniform and it is no derogation of God's faithfulness if a spiritual precept built upon them proves to all appearances unfruitful. That saving faithfulness of God which religion embraces is not found in the infallibility of the precepts but in the maintenance of the saving relation. The man who remains constant to the divine friendship is blessed by being progressively broken in and united to the action of God, whatever pains or disappointments the process involves. The last pain is death; and the collapse of the psychosomatic person, with all its functions, arts and precepts may be either instantaneous or agonisingly gradual. Since we cannot directly experience here the maintenance or restoration of the relationship beyond this life, the final verification of divine fidelity escapes us. We are considering the experiential grounds of belief, and all we can say is that the believer is content with the evidence he has. While and in so far as his person remains intact, his prayers are (in his own view) not unanswered, though in the direct form they are disappointed. For their main intention is union of will, and this the divine action deepens, if the man will accept it. From such a union, and from it alone, the blessings of sanctity spring. The blessings are manifold—there is not only the sheer fact of harmony with our Creator, there is the participation in his acts, purposes and affections, so far as it concerns us to enter into them.

In giving this brief phenomenology of a certain aspect of religious belief I have done my best to be objective and not to make a sermon. I can only hope that I have said enough and no more than enough for the purpose we have in hand—to consider the applicability of empirical principles to the religion we seriously hold. We will proceed now to ask a few straightforward questions on this head.

Is theological belief an idle speculation, leaving our action unengaged?—By this account, plainly not.—What can we do about God?—We can devote ourselves to his will; that is, we can place ourselves in his action as we suppose it to be disclosed.—Is there any empirical verification of our engagement with the actual will of an actual God?—Only of a general kind, in so far as we find 'life' or 'blessing' in the process, through God's uniting us with his will; and when we say 'with his will' we are saying 'with himself'. No gulf opens in the empirical argument between the will of God, and God. If 'God's will' means 'God's voluntary action' then it is a synonym for God himself; for what is a person but his voluntary action? Finite persons, indeed, such as we are, are so imperfectly integrated that they have no full possession of themselves and are not wholly in their acts; but such qualifications seem meaningless when transferred to God, and in any case play no part in the religious fact. 'God's will' can, of course, be given a meaning which makes it other than God himself; it can be made to stand for 'that which God intends'. Thus bad and heedless men may fulfil God's will while intending the very opposite. But I hope it is plain that the engagement with God's will, which we have attempted to describe, is not of this exterior kind.

Little if anything is to be gained by fighting a pitched philosophical battle over the blessed word 'empirical'. Let every reader add up the score for himself, and decide whether to accord religious evidence the creditable epithet. 'Pseudo-empirical' will be the verdict of the unbeliever; the believer may say 'As empirical as the matter allows—and how could God give us more to do about himself than he gives, or how, being God, make a more verificatory response to what he lets us do?'— 'Oh yes, he very well might,' another may say, taking up the last point, and opening a very long discussion. But that discussion would be essentially theological, not philosophic. For it would concern what it might have beseemed God to do. Would he have done better so to relate us to himself as to put faith less upon the stretch, so that (for example) Christ's 'learning obedience by the things he' (unpredictably) 'suffered' would cease to be the paradigm of faith?

If the wrangle over 'empirical' appears important, it is presumably because of the relation empirical evidence is held to bear towards the assertion of existence; so a passing remark on that relation will not be out of place here.

If we are getting reactions of any kind out of our environment, then no doubt something exists there; but so vague an assertion is of no interest and no one would ever bother to make it. If, on occasions arranged by us, we can obtain reactions of a foreseen kind, we can assert the existence of that which has the character of so acting on such occasions; and this is supposed to be a typical assertion of existence. A moment's reflection will show that it is nothing of the sort. A physical assertion, however experimentally verified, assures us primarily of a systematically intelligible item in our field of physical contacts. It assures us secondarily of real finite activities or energies such as to produce an interaction-event of the kind. But, as is notorious, we get further and further out of our depth if we try to pinpoint the unitary components of such energies, or to conceive what sort of an existence they have. Nor is that all. A physical assertion is not only an indirect, not only a vague assertion of physical realities; it can afford to be and ought to be an agnostic one. Let the realities be what they may, they jointly exercise the force of which the regular effect can be controlled by us.

A physical assertion does not, except through carelessness or superstition, assert any existent reality having any definite mode of existence. And why does not it? Because the physical ultimates, whatever they may be, are nothing to us. We are not called upon to do anything about them. By contrast take the case of a biological organism. There is nothing specially privileged about the evidence which assures me that it is a stable and going pattern. It is empirical evidence like any other. But suppose this organism comes within the sweep of some clearance I am making, and I nevertheless decide to spare it; not because it happens to be a subject of pleasure or curiosity to me, but because it seems a shame not to let it carry on. Then unless my decision is a piece of whimsical make-believe, I am placing a value on the organism which implies that it is something in itself; that the statement 'no creature would be destroyed by the resolution of this complex into its elements' is false. To take an extreme case: a philosopher who claims to believe that human existence is a mere assemblage or sequence of momentary pyschic atoms risks his life to save a drowning stranger. Though the inconsistency can be talked away by use of a great many words, good sense will judge that his action refutes his theory. His deed affirms the value of the stranger as existent; for by asserting the value he asserts the subject on which the value is pinned.

A decision about intrinsic value is not a decision about existence; but the intrinsic values of existing being make claims on us of a distinct and unmistakable kind, and to admit the claim is to assert the existence. Not that the value of anything can be the *evidence* for its existence; whatever we value as real must present itself to us in some way, before we can set a value on it. Language may mislead us here. We can say if we like that we know God through his goodness and through nothing else; but only if 'God's goodness' means 'his active benevolence' or something of that sort. If 'God's goodness' means the excellent character of the life which he enjoys or rather, which he is, how are we to believe in him on the ground of it? He would not even have become an object to our minds in the first place.

Value cannot substitute for evidence; what it can do is to force us to judge it. Let the evidence of an existence be in some way obscure or difficult to assess by the customary rules. Then the intrinsic value of the existent which the evidence would prove if the evidence were sound, forces on us the effort of judging whether it is sound or not; always supposing the value would be one that would make claims on our action. And so it has always been recognised that faith in God calls for voluntary effort; we could spare the trouble of deciding so mysterious and unique an issue, were it not that the absolute value of the Being involved obliges us to the exertion.

So, then, empirical evidence as such does not lead to serious assertions of existence without an accompanying acknowledgement of value. Value and existence together are most emphatically asserted by appropriate action. And the value-question makes the existence-question urgent.

Let us hope that these hasty remarks will have served to place the question about empirical verification in perspective. For one perspective, one unbroken context embraces the value-principle and the verification-principle. They find their places in the whole of action. I test environmental activities by seeing what I can do with them. I determine what I think of environing agents by deciding what to do about them. God is not to be placed in our environment; but *mutatis mutandis*, the two sides of active assessment which relate us to our environment are also present in our knowledge of God.

The mere assertion of something existent or actual in our environment is of metaphysical interest only; it finds its place, for example, in an argument against Berkeleianism. Physical assertion begins to be of common interest when it tells us where a certain energy or a certain resistance is to be met, and what it can be expected to do. So equally with asserting the existence of God. The bare assertion belongs to a dispute against metaphysical atheism. Practical assertions concern God's particular action. Not but that the action-reference may be indirect. We may seem to be saying something of vast importance when we assert the divine attributes; and if the assertion of the attributes is felt to be implicit already in the assertion of the existence, the practical importance will inhere in that assertion too. But the practical significance of the attributes lies in the particular actions they imply. God's power, wisdom and goodness are taken to bear manifold fruit in his creation; they mean that he will everywhere do effectively and wisely what is best. General active tendencies are of no significance where there is no particular action; least of all as attributed to God, whose activity cannot be supposed ever to be out of exercise.

When we were speaking of empirical verification in relation

to God's action we said that it could be called no more than general; but this was not to say that the action verified is general; the notion is really meaningless. We can talk about the general action of a law, either civil or natural; but this is to speak by metaphor. A law does not act; a multitude of agents, whether physical agents or *agents de police*, act in conformity with it. Or again, a real action may have a general effect, as when I scatter water from a watering-can. But the action is particular.

If God acts in this world, he acts particularly; and if I had no conception of the particular lines along which his purpose works, and were not ready to experiment with my guesses, I could not associate my action with the divine and the whole scheme of religion as we have set it out falls to the ground. And anyhow it is plain that Christians attribute many particular actions and many particular purposes to the divine will; and hold that they would be shown many more, had they but the perceptiveness to see them.

The question, how we make out or identify the line of the divine action, is a question of detail, of practice, and of day-to-day religion. A more obviously general and philosophic problem is how to conceive the relation between the divine action and the activities of created agents. Reflection on the relation goes back to the classic age of Israelite prophecy, if it goes no further. Isaiah was convinced that the Assyrian invasions were the scourge of God, a Father's correction of his sons' rebellion. But he knew that the Assyrians were not somnambulists under a divine hypnotism. The Assyrian was a rod in the hand of God's indignation, but he had no notion of being anything of the kind. His motives were acquisitive or political. If we can make out a prophetic theory about the mechanism of the divine control, it lies in the openness of men's thoughts to pressures of which they are unaware. The Assyrian feels the force of the reasons for harsh action against Judaea; but the reasons might not have occurred to him, or an alternative use of his troops might have seemed more rewarding. The hearts of kings are in God's rule and governance; he turns them as it seems best to his godly wisdom.

To take the matter a stage further—how did the prophet suppose that the divine influence came to bear? Perhaps it is unjust to treat pictorial language as philosophical theory; but one can only say that the Hebrews were ready to talk about the Breath of the Lord as though it were a finite force, an agent among agents, moving the cogitations of the heart as the wind sways the trees. It needs no words to show that such an idea is impossible to us as anything but poetry.

We may say of the Hebrews, that they commonly saw divine effects as having creaturely agents, but found it needless to enquire how the divine hand wielded its instruments; they were content to use the simplest pictures. And the modern Christian is really in no worse or better case. He begins with the assumption that certain events, within himself or without, are divine effects. He does not doubt that they are the immediate act of natural agents, for if they were not, how would they be in this world of ours at all? If he speculates on the way in which the divine control takes effect, he probably goes no further than to tell himself that there is room for it to act; for the grid of causal uniformity does not (to any evidence) fit so tight upon natural processes as to bar the influence of an over-riding divine persuasion. If asked what on earth he can mean by 'persuasion' or 'influence' in such a connexion, he may simply refuse the challenge. What sense is there in demanding an exact account of an action which, by hypothesis, is outside our knowledge?

If he is up in traditional philosophy he can elaborate his refusal by an appeal to the doctrine of analogy. According to this doctrine, we *believe* that God's way of acting is the infinitely higher analogue of our way, but we cannot *conceive* it otherwise than in terms of our own. God's agency must actually be such as to work omnipotently on, in, or through creaturely agencies without either forcing them or competing with them. But as soon as we try to conceive it in action, we degrade it to the creaturely level and place it in the field of interacting causalities. The result can only be (if we take it literally) monstrosity and confusion.

The argument is painfully negative and prompts the retort: 'You have shown me why the idea of a First Cause cannot be expected to work. I should have thought this to be a good reason for discarding it. What can you do with a First Cause which stands in no workable relation to second causes? You are blocked at the first move you have to make.' There may be several counters to this objection; heaven knows there are few finalities in metaphysical dispute. But the best counter is surely the practical one. It can be shown that the direct relating of finite causal agency to divine action is a task which, in our living concern with the divine, we never attempt, and have no means of placing in a practical light.

The first point to be observed is that God's agency does not strike us in the springing-point of causes but in the finished effect. Isaiah does not begin from a speculation into the mystery of Assyrian motives, but from the divine act of scourging Israel's back with an Assyrian rod. His reference of the effect to its divine cause does not go by way of the Assyrian's choices even though he turns aside to muse upon them. The religious mind goes direct from the divine handiwork to the divine maker; it is like the amateur's identification of a work of art. This, he says, is surely a Rembrandt; in style, merit and feeling it is his. He knows nothing of Rembrandt's methods. Let us suppose that the picture is an ideal composition. Did the artist paint out of his head, or did he set the scene with models dressed and posed, and the light carefully arranged? How many basic pigments did he use, and how did he lay his brush-strokes? Did he follow set precepts or recipes in the grouping of shapes and colours? Here are questions which the art-historian can very likely answer, but in which the amateur may be utterly at sea; and yet he may be talking good sense when he says 'This is a Rembrandt'.

If we ask how the amateur knows, we realise at once that he cannot compare the painter's art or mind with his picture, so as to judge the second worthy of the first. The painter's artistry is not an experienceable object. Our amateur can but judge from authentic pictures already studied. Yet to say this is not to say that Rembrandt and his artistry are superfluous terms, interrupting a comparative study of actual pictures. For what one judges is not simply that the newly-met picture is formally like its brothers. One judges that the likenesses and unlikenesses too are such that a man who had painted the acknowledged canvases might have painted this one also. And when we so judge we draw on our understanding of human inventiveness and of human purpose; we know how creative minds in any field like to vary their inventions; we have judged from his acknowledged canvases how Rembrandt liked to vary his. It is true enough that the amateur works from the pictures he knows; yet he uses them as evidence for answering the question what Rembrandt might paint, and whether he painted this; referring to Rembrandt's artistry the completed product, not the steps traversed in producing it; for of these we are supposing our amateur to be ignorant.

The application of the parable scarcely needs drawing out. A Christian has his accepted works of the divine hand, which give him his types of Providence in action. In view of these he appreciates the ever-new works of God. And his appreciation is of achievement, not technique; in the terms of our parable, he is inescapably amateur.

He is so, for no accidental reason. The artistic amateur could become an art-historian and pry into technique; the religious mind cannot do anything of the sort. The practical relation of his action to God's is one which does not allow the technical question to arise.

Let us consider the religious predicament. We are faced with the work of God. Speculatively we shall hold that it embraces whatever happens. Practically we are concerned with a drift of divine action both manifest to us and involving our own. There is no escaping in this connexion the analogy offered by our neighbour's conduct and our need to interpret it. That our neighbour does act, there is no question; we see the signs of it in the movements of his body. The question is, what he is at, and how it concerns us. For the purpose of the comparison we are making, the whole world of events must be said to compose the bodily motions of the divine will. Measured by the mighty mass, the divine purpose (we must confess) is sparingly signified to us.

My neighbour's conduct bears upon me as a finite system of action, basically physical, with which I have to engage the similar system of my own. It is so, whether my concern is to fit into his plans or to fit him into mine. Merely to establish communication with him I must work my throat, and make impressions on his ears; the bodily relation is simply reversed, if I submit to his direction or advice. In all our cooperation with our neighbour something happens, of which the engagement of one cog-wheel with another is a tolerable diagram. Whereas in the engagement of our action with God's there is no sort of parallel to any of this. We are concerned with his purpose and action solely as an operation to which we commit ourselves. It is no part of our business to work any determinate system of communication. We do not find where and by what means to touch God nor where and by what means to undergo his touch. We enter into his action simply by acting, whether the action be a movement of thought or an employment of the hand. We believe, and even claim to find, that his action sustains or inspires ours; but the divine assistance is experienced simply in its effect. To be assisted by a mountaineer I must put my weight on a rope; to receive the divine assistance I have only to think or act my trust in God.

I know that I am retailing the very platitude of spiritual religion. Perhaps the consequence I propose to draw has not been so generally remarked. It is that the causal joint (so to speak) between infinite and finite action plays and in the nature of the case can play no part in our concern with God and his will. We can do nothing about it, nor does it bear on anything that we can do. And so, on empirical ground, the question about it is a question which does not arise and may be condemned as no question at all. Without finding the causal joint between my action-system and my neighbours', still more evidently, between my action-system and inanimate environmental systems, I cannot relate my action to theirs or theirs to mine. The causal joint (could there be said to be one) between God's action and ours is of no concern in the activity of religion; the very idea of it arises simply as a by-product of the analogical imagination, as we explained above. Surely it is nothing new that imagination should fall over its own feet, or symbolism tangle into knots.

Turn from symbolism to action, and the problem vanishes. We can, in the only possible way, experience the active relation of a created energy to the Creator's action by embracing the divine will. Everyone who prays knows that the object of the exercise is a thought or an aspiration or a caring which is no more ours than it is that of God in us. The philosopher who sets out to examine the religious fact, and who brushes away such an account of prayer as mere *Schwaermerei* or pious rant,[1] may as well close the enquiry at once. He has said his last word; the whole thing's nonsense. Let him devote his attention to a more serious topic.

The position which we have outlined, if it is accepted, carries some significant corollaries. First, the vanishing of the problem of freewill and divine predestination in the achievement of salvation. We know that the action of a man can be the action of God in him; our religious existence is an experimenting with this relation. Both the divine and the human actions remain real and therefore free in the union between them; not knowing the modality of the divine action we cannot pose the problem of their mutual relation. All a spiritual guide need do is append anathema to any proposition which denies the personal reality of either the human action or the divine, or which, admitting both, inverts the hierarchy and makes the divine action conse- quent upon the human rather than *vice versa*.

A second corollary is that Grace ceases to be a special problem

---

[1] Many philosophers would see themselves excused from examining any such account by the supposed demonstration that a reference of human duty to divine will is either vacuous or immoral. For an examination of this argu- ment see Mr. B. G. Mitchell's forthcoming book, *Religion and Morals*.

or even a special concept. It is superfluous to postulate a super-naturalising extra imparted to the creature, and unnecessary to take refuge by way of reaction in the shallow description of Grace as mere influence. Grace is an action of the Creator in the creature. He acts in the creature everywhere; when he acts in the rational creature he is pleased to act in that creature's mental and voluntary life, bringing them into his own. For of such a conformity or union with the divine, mind and will can be made capable. Physical or animal energies cannot.

CHAPTER V

NATURE AND CREATION

WE concentrated in our last chapter on the relation between human action and divine action, as day-to-day religion knows it. We left undeveloped the topic of what forms divine action may take. We insisted on two points only: that divine action, to be real, must be particular; and that our appreciations of its particular drift are not in detail verifiable. The impression left on one's mind by such contentions might well be that of a simple old-fashioned piety, moving in a world of special providences confidently asserted and comically reassessed. Mr Jones's rheumatism was a judgment, until his daughter swore to you on the bible that the tale about his secret drinking was a baseless slander. Her father was a saint. His rheumatism, therefore, was a trial. But then the bowling-club went on a day's outing and drove their charabanc into the sea; and Mr Jones's rheumatism, since it kept him at home on the occasion, proved a blessing in disguise, and a providence indeed.

What sort of divine government was this? *Le père de famille est capable de tout*, the domestic autocrat might practise on the characters of his household in some such spirit. Make him metaphysically *capable de tout*, endow him with omnipotence, and you have the god of kicks and halfpence. In a former chapter we considered the use and abuse of human parable as applied to things divine. We saw the danger of so pressing the personal image as to forbid the facts to speak for themselves. The petty providentialism we have caricatured is refuted by the simple observation that it goes against the grain of fact. Suppose a mind on the one hand possessed by a lively sense of God's benevolence and endowed on the other with a keen eye for the realities of existence. Who can conceive such a mind's reaching the un-biassed judgment that the form taken by God's good govern-ment in this world was the form exemplified in the little drama of Mr Jones's rheumatism?

If we are to go with the grain of fact, God must be the God of nature; 'nature' being no more than a name for the grain of fact, at every level below intelligent choice. The natural sets the whole stage for the personal, and the natural penetrates the personal at every point. Mr Jones's rheumatism is a natural fact, a natural accident to a natural body. It may be that God 'overrules' natural effects for the benefit of such as Mr Jones; he cannot be supposed to create a nature, for the sole purpose of twisting it to ulterior ends. Nature has its own validity, and before we can ask how it is overruled we must see how it is ruled.

It has been taught by out-and-out theological dogmatists that God's creation and government of nature are truths received by way of revelation and otherwise uncertified. Isaiah proclaimed them, Christ concurred in them; there's no more to be said. Any claim on behalf of the ungodly heathen to have possessed these doctrines independently is brushed aside; when they said 'God' they didn't mean 'God' and when they said 'create' they didn't mean 'create'. It is difficult for a philosopher to see what a dogmatism of this sort amounts to, or on what ground it can be supposed to stand. But like other outrages on commonsense, it has the merit of provoking reflection; and I will make a remark or two upon it.

First, the substance of revelation might seem to lie in a special action of God for the redemption and blessing of his rational creatures, an action going quite beyond any working of nature; and while such a special action can scarcely fail to cast light on the natural order, the light so cast will surely be marginal to the focus of the revealing act. Revelation may be said to institute an order of grace; it cannot institute the order of nature, but at the most illuminate it. The dogma we are criticising may be deemed harmless, if it teaches that revelation gives us eyes to see what is there, and directs us, so gifted, to look in front of our noses. For in that case it will throw us on the natural order and move us to go with the grain of fact. If, on the other hand, the dogma means that we are not to look in nature for the God of nature, but to plant on her a dogmatic *a priori*, then the dogma becomes a serious matter and, surely, a serious nuisance.

Taken in the sense we have called harmless, it may be viewed as an intransigently Christian expression of the approach we wish to commend. The only God who can mean anything to the human mind is the God about whom the human will has something to do. Now the revelation which institutes the Order of Grace determines for Christians what they have to do in face of God, by determining the nature of his saving action towards them. When Christians look at natural providence, it will be to learn more about the action of the God they worship. But surely a man who has a living practice of some other religion may look for his God in the natural field, taking his start from whatever pattern of interaction with the divine his religion knows. If we take the widest area of induction, and survey the religion of mankind, it would seem that a commerce with saving, or propitiation of threatening powers comes first; somewhat shadowy speculations about the origin of the habitable world are widespread at a comparatively early level of development; they are not the centre of concern and their integration with vital cult is a later achievement. Religion begins in a direct relation with divine power, and comes at length to feel it in its root at the origin of the natural world.

If we do approach the theology of nature from the side of practical religion, we may hope to run a middle course through the straits of philosophical danger. The Charybdis of the enquiry is the abyss of vacuity. If to assert a divine government is merely to say that nature goes on being natural, theism adds nothing to naturalism. Of course nature's natural; what else could it be? To be sure of shunning our Charybdis, we are driven to say that the divine government makes nature more than natural, by bringing natural forces into combinations of achievement they would not of themselves attain. Only then we run on Scylla, the impossibility of verification. It is an old tale; a word is enough to recall it. Gardens show evidence of the gardener's hand, because nature is not left to go its own way. Eden might have proved a ruling providence, but what of the sort can be evidenced by this world of ours, where Adam in the sweat of his brow must fight with thorns and thistles?

Like Homer's hero, we must give Charybdis a wide birth and go closer to Scylla; but how are we to scrape by? Let us make a brief critical examination of this 'impossibility of verification'. If we cannot show that nature does more than what comes naturally, why cannot we? Our inability might be due either to knowledge or to ignorance. To knowledge, if we have reason to think that nature contains resources of power and principles of action sufficient for all the order and intricacy we find in things; to ignorance, if we are simply in no position to argue one way or the other. We shall proceed to defend the agnostic alternative.

If any sense is to be made of the question it must be understood as ontological. We are talking about the actual components of the world, whatever they may be. For want of a better name, we will call them natural agencies. Now we take it as historical fact that higher or more organised systems have emerged from the more elementary. On that supposition we can take an elementary state of affairs at a level arbitrarily chosen and ask whether the agencies whose interaction constitutes that state of affairs will of themselves produce higher systems such as we observe, under the pressure of disturbances which naturally or accidentally arise.

Such is the question we have to ask; and it is surely plain that we cannot answer it. Our knowledge of physical being can never be close enough. All we can know will be generalised laws governing the interactions of our 'natural agencies'. The business of the scientific enquirer will be to formulate uniformities of natural action and he can look for them everywhere. If he takes the flat-rate principle of a given level, then of course he confines his account of things to that level. If he takes the principle of a higher-level uniformity, it will, once more, be proper to the level taken. But he can also bridge between the levels in several ways. First, he can show that lower-level uniformities continue to operate in the constituents of higher-level patterns. Second, that the build-up of lower into higher follows rules not singular to the case but common to the known natural world. And third, that wide generalisations can be framed to cover the working of lower-level uniformities, higher-level uniformities, and uniformities of transition or build-up from level to level.

Suppose all these scientific tasks performed to our entire satisfaction, what light will have been cast on our ontological question—the question whether the agencies responsible for a low-level system had it in them to produce higher-level systems without a Creator's aid? All that will have been shown is that whatever happens does not happen inconsistently; whether the consistent action is that of natural agencies unaided, or natural agencies divinely supported, will not have been shown at all. If we knew *either* that natural agencies left to themselves would act chaotically *or* that natural agencies divinely overruled would act whimsically, then the orderliness we observe in nature would vote for or against divine assistance. The first supposition is scarcely worth considering, and as for the second, it is not likely to recommend itself to believers who approach nature from their experience of grace. *Gratia perficit naturam, non tollit,* and it will be analogously expected that creative aid should enable natural agencies to go beyond themselves in their own way, the way of uniformity; a way neither imposed on nature, nor interrupted in nature, by the supervenient and perfecting act of God.

It would follow that no scientific arguments or discoveries tell either for or against the thesis that natural agencies need divine assistance to do what they actually do. There is a theological supposition in this field on which empirical considerations come to bear, but that is the supposition of miracle. The medical observers at Lourdes do their best to establish whether the cures which take place fall within or without the limits of natural analogy; that is, whether any reasonable extension of accepted uniformities will cover them. Medical arguments are not indeed conclusive in proving a miracle, but neither are they irrelevant. The medical investigator at least knows how to go about his task. Ask him to enquire whether natural processes of cure themselves require a divine assistance of natural forces, and he will know neither how to begin nor what to look for.

Our question is not a scientific question; but granted that we can talk ontology at all, it is not an absurd one. If we suppose an infinity of very simple packets or systems of energy each active according to the principle of its kind, and then ask whether the world we know can or will result from their action without an assisting cause, 'Why on earth not?' isn't so obvious an answer as to foreclose discussion. If we refuse the theistic hypothesis in any form, we shall have to hold some queer and surprising views, either about the effect of accidental combination, or about the latent powers of our basic natural elements.

'Never mind,' it may be rejoined; 'why not queer implications about what we cannot bring into the focus of observation nor handle by any practice or technique? In such a penumbra of the intelligible, how is one to decide what is queer and what is not? There is a vast and developing manifold of agencies which engages our action. We can pick out uniformities *ad infinitum* from the interaction-patterns; but what is the use of speculating on ultimate interagents, which we can never perfectly isolate, still less adequately define?'

This objection raises the whole question of the profitableness of metaphysical discussion as such, a question about which opinion has greatly fluctuated even in my working lifetime. I suppose that many philosophers would now agree that to discuss the ontology of nature may be a healthy exercise as long as we do not attach the wrong kind of importance to it. The inconclusive war of rival hypotheses will make us see what sort of mysteriousness attaches to realities which we constantly touch but never fully grasp. The elusiveness of ultimates will be revealed—indeed will be defined—by the mutual destruction of the best theses we can state about them. If we find people inclining to stand on one thesis rather than on its contrary (for example, on the thesis that nature is assisted or shaped by a higher cause) it will be for other reasons than those arising out of the metaphysical game. There will be practical implications; attachments of some kind between the thesis preferred and issues arising in the field of action.

Those who accept any such account of metaphysical activity as we have just sketched will be virtually agreeing that Kant's treatment of the matter remains classical, for all the maddening admixture of perversity in his arguments. But if Kant's position stands, it is only in its main lines. There is nothing like a common orthodoxy as to which the practical attitudes or activities are, that anchor ·floating metaphysical theses to the rock of solid experience. Kant put forward several suggestions; our contemporaries have sponsored others. I do not want to make an inventory of philosophers' opinions. There is one decisive line of cleavage running across them all. Either they make the practical attachments of the thesis such as to constitute a serious affirmation of it, or they do not. The gentle agnosticism of philosophical minds inclines to the weak alternative. A philosophy which is Christian in any traditional sense seems committed to the stronger.

To illustrate the distinction of weak and strong, let us take up again the famous parable of the invisible gardener. If it has a gardener, the natural world is a wild garden laid out with so skilful and so self-effacing an informality that the gardener's hand can never be convincingly detected in any single feature. If we are nevertheless moved to affirm a gardener, what attaches us to the idea? Many answers of the 'weak' type can readily be given. They fall into two main classes: illusions of projection and contextual encouragements.

Illusions of projection may find their paradigm in Michaelangelo's famous remark, that he thought of the figure he was to cut as buried in the block of marble, only asking to be disinterred by the chisel. We can easily shift the application to a different part of the aesthetic field. To enjoy a finished work of art is to appreciate a pattern put there by the artist; to enjoy a natural landscape is to pick out a pattern for oneself. It is an unquestioned fact that wild nature offers materials for a pattern-finding activity in our minds and senses. It does not follow that nature has been aesthetically composed for our or any observer's benefit. To suppose a divine landscape-gardener may be a myth inclining us to a suitable enjoyment of natural scenes; it can scarcely on this evidence be anything better. A more serious projection is the scientific, where the patterns we suppose prefigured by divine handiwork are the systems in which we collect the manifold of natural fact. It may dispose us suitably for our scientific task to approach the world as though created by a cosmic engineer endowed with the mind of a mathematical physicist; but seriously to assert the existence of such a person would (on the evidence) be going far.

So much for 'illusions of projection'. We have called the other branch of a weak involvement with metaphysical assertion 'contextual encouragement'. This is where the metaphysical supposition is more or less directly related to what we do. We see ourselves no longer as mooning about the garden of nature, whether to admire or to describe it. We take our spades and fall to gardening on our own account; and we find it an encouragement to place our efforts in a setting of supposed cosmic action.

There are several ways in which the universal gardener's work may be felt to provide an encouraging context for our own endeavours. The crudest is a mere support to the hope of success. Adam in the sweat of his brow must fight down thistles and raise corn for his bread. It comforts him to believe that a creative purpose works towards corn-harvest, having merely delegated the tasks of ploughing, weeding and sowing to human hands; that (to parody Matthew Arnold) there is a power not ourselves making for nutriment.

A more refined concern is with the appropriateness of our action. The issue comes into view as soon as the bare necessities of life have been met and we have some scope of choice. We find ourselves in effect deciding what sort of life we shall make for ourselves and what sort of shape we shall impose on our environment. We are in a sense creating, but we are not creating *in vacuo*. What we design must be not only good in itself; it must make one worthy whole with the nature it develops or on which it builds. And so we may view ourselves as a sort of landscape-gardeners; like Mr Milestone or Capability Brown, we see that the hill calls for a crown of trees if it is really to be itself, and that the brook, to make its due effect, cries out for dams, pools and cataracts. There's a power not ourselves making for the picturesque.

The parable we are following has, I fear, misled us into flippancy. If we reflect that the nature upon which we practise will be chiefly that of our fellow-creatures we shall see that it is no laughing matter. We cannot be free to do to them just what suits us; when due consideration has been given to their conscious wishes, we would be happy to foster their intrinsic capacities, to go with the grain of their nature. The conception of a creative purpose to be obeyed or assisted is of real moral value here—a power not ourselves making for rightness.

A third sort of concern is closely linked with the second, concern for unity of purpose with our fellows. Free agreement on what it might be good freely to construct seems unattainable in a parliament of mankind, unless we may suppose a divine purpose in nature itself, reaching out into the field of human invention and of human endeavour; a purpose of which we may hope jointly to become aware; a power not ourselves, making for concord.

If we glance back over the illusions of projection and the contextual encouragements, it seems evident that the latter attach us more seriously, and come nearer to religious belief, than do the former. Kant said as much—indeed, he said more; he exaggerated the difference to the point of making contextual encouragement the substance of religious conviction. By means of special pleas which are unlikely to persuade us, he argued that no reflective man could act with full moral seriousness without admitting a divine control over nature. His method of reasoning is so singular that to mention him may seem an irrelevance; yet it is difficult to pass in silence so famous an example.

Whatever his special arguments, it seems fair to say that Kant failed to convince his philosophical posterity of the absolute line he drew between illusions of projection and contextual encouragements. It seems plain without more words that neither form of attachment to a metaphysical thesis involves an affirmation of it. To look, to think, to act *as though* God were keeping the ring for our efforts does not commit us to theistic belief. It may well be that we cannot enjoy the comforts of contextual support without a solid belief in God based on other grounds; but if such grounds are not forthcoming, the moral will be that we must do without the comforts of contextual support; not that contextual considerations can be made to take the weight of belief.

When contextual motives are put forward as *the* motives of religious affirmation, a believer can scarcely fail to see what is happening. He is familiar with the attitude of benevolent neutrality towards his faith; an attitude which, withholding commitment, allows the maintenance of ceremonial religion and the currency of pious language; cultural forms taken to provide a happy context for men's autonomous activities. He cannot be slow to recognise contextual theories of religious attachment as nothing more nor less than philosophical elaborations of the neutralist position. To a believing eye, they all read like attempts to define the market by listing the sideshows; accounts of religion which leave religion out.

The believer's attachment to his metaphysical thesis is not contextual but direct. Knowing, as he claims to do, the God of Grace, he relates himself to a will already operative through the process of nature. His initial concern is to know what God is doing, not what sense man can make of the natural world, either by interpreting it or by actively developing it. The personal doing which attaches him to his thesis about nature is his dealing with the God of nature. We will not repeat here that we wrote in a former chapter about the substance of religion.

If it be asked how the believer is to pick out the gold thread of divine intention from the web of natural events, we may toss the question back to the contextualists. If there are no seemings of divine purpose in nature, what becomes of the contextual theory? The believer takes the seemings for fact, though most ready (if he is wise) to admit the fallibility of his detailed recognitions.

There need be nothing fanciful in a religious attitude to nature. We can adhere to the main lines of creative process; can see the hand of God in the making of individual systems, of creatures or races of creatures; can be sparing of judgments on the providential bearing of chance and accident besetting them. To return to our beginning, Mr Jones in all his rugged individuality is the work of God's hand; and but for the special accidents of his life he would not be what he is. But we may let ourselves off assigning a special intention to the incidence of his rheumatism.

Here is a subject on which I have perpetrated a book called 'Love Almighty and Ills Unlimited'. Whether it is good or bad, I cannot yet see my way to making it much better, and I excuse myself from either quoting it or paraphrasing it. It will be more to our present purpose to take up a different topic.

When we were discussing the activity of religion, we laid it down on empirical or pragmatic grounds that the causal joint (as it were) between divine action and creaturely action can never be anything to us. More recently, discussing the metaphysics of nature, we have laid down a negative which seems to run parallel; that we can never put our finger on a point at which natural agencies without divine assistance must fail of their observed effects. In form, the parallel is apparent. How far is it a parallel of substance? We may consider first the issue raised in either case, and second the reason in either case for our inability to come to grips with the issue.

The neatest way to put the similarity of the issues raised is to indulge a little mythology. Let us endow the ultimate component of natural force—the Whatever-it-is in Itself behind the electron—with a Christian soul. The minute creature may then be supposed to stand in the same relation to God's action by way of nature, as does the Christian to God's action by way of grace. It can throw itself on a creative purpose which carries it beyond itself; but has (presumably) as little concern as we have with the causal touch through which the divine action embraces, directs or extends that of the creature. Now let us cancel the mythical supposition. The minute entity has neither mind nor will; yet the causal or quasi-causal relation between it and infinite purpose may be thought the same in principle as the causal dependence of our action upon the divine.

Now to compare the grounds of ignorance in the two cases. The parallel would be oddly balanced if the one reason lay in the intrinsic nature of the religious activity while the other rested on particular conclusions of physical enquiry; if the one reason were 'philosophical' and the other 'scientific'. But it is not so. The present-day picture of the elusiveness of physical ultimates is no mere hypothesis prompted by experimental results. It is true that experimental progress has driven scientists to abandon older and cruder tenets about the basic constituents of nature. But the older tenets were always nonsensical and should have been exploded (they sometimes were) on philosophical grounds. The progress of science has but brought the intrinsic limits of enquiry into view. Those limits are set, not by the present reach of our experiments, but by the nature of our physical experience. We know natural agents by their interaction with us and therefore cannot extract a purely objective account of them.

On both sides, then, the ground of ignorance lies in the limited nature of an active relation—in the one case our relation with God's will, in the other our relation with physical activities. So far so good; but it has still to be admitted that the parallel is crookedly drawn. We can see this at a glance by constructing in the spiritual sphere the proper parallel to what we have in the natural. We cannot press a knowledge of physical agencies far enough to say that they are capable of just so much, and the extra is divine. But neither can we press a knowledge of human capacities so far as to say, 'Man stops here; it is God who makes the saint.' Here are two causes of ignorance equally negative; neither leaves us with any ground on which to affirm theology or to deny it. The reason we previously gave for ignorance of spiritual causality was theologically positive. We have a real commerce with real deity, and it is such as to exclude our having any business with an infinite-finite causal joint. We cannot give a similarly positive reason for our ignorance of God's physical causality; for we do not touch God with our fingers as we touch him with our 'souls'.

Never mind; the divine action with which we make spiritual contact is all one in the natural and in the spiritual world; its roots run right down. Man himself is a microcosm, a little summary of creation, his roots in the bottom of the physical, his flower of life in knowledge, choice and love. If the God I know is no more than the God of me, he is a God who builds me from my basic clay and sets me in the Eden of my effective environment; and that is no small fragment of a universe.

Religious concern being with the actual will of God as it affects us, faith will affirm God's direction of nature before she comes to the ultimate mystery, the creation of all from nothing. But she has only to persevere in the same path in order to reach it. If it is the work of God which educes higher levels of action out of lower, so that the higher which were not come to be, then it does not seem that any leve can pass muster as simple fact. What privilege of status has the lowest or most elementary organisation of physical agency that we can either detect or conceive? That nothing more elementary could be is no reason why anything so elementary should be, unless the Will that works up through all levels was pleased to start from the bottom. The will of God, once admitted, cannot be limited by anything pre-existent to his action; he must be the first, total and sufficient cause.

The purpose of what we have just said extends no further than to find a place for the doctrine of creation in the religious affirmation of one divine action through creation, nature and grace. The analysis of such an idea as sheer creation, and the offering either of analogies to illuminate or of arguments to commend it, are tasks to fill volumes. We have done nothing to ease an approach to such a mystery except to suggest that it may be most naturally reached by a backward extrapolation from physical Providence. Not that, abstractly considered, the divine government of nature is vastly more intelligible to us than sheer creation; only that it is more real, as more directly engaging our religious action. We do not and cannot do anything about God's creating, until it prolongs itself into a developing or fostering of his creatures. Then it begins to engage our duty or our desire.

In treating of God's work in nature we skirted the territory of positive science, and touched upon experimentally verified conclusions. We find ourselves on similar ground when we come to creation. It is commonly taught by Christian philosophers that the argument for creation is indifferent to changes in physical theory; for it rests on an ontological insufficiency in the finite as such, which no physical theory either asserts or denies. We do not wish to quarrel with this contention; but however it may be with the argument for a creation, it ought not to be said that our manner of conceiving the creative act remains unaffected by physical theory.

We can make the point clear by comparing scholastic times with our own. In the view of the Aristotelian physicist, nothing corporeal need either move or act in order to be itself. A substance could simply exist, without actualising either its inherent susceptibilities to causal influence, or its inherent capacities for responsive action. If the appropriate influences came to bear, it would be time for it to make the corresponding responses.

Such a physical doctrine allowed the theologian a picture of creation drawn in accordance with it. God creates the substances. But shall they act? They shall. The God who made them ordains that a spiritual influence shall touch the stars, responsive to which they turn themselves in their several spheres. From their movements influence passes down through level after level, and what would else have been a Sleeping Beauty's palace wakes into life.

How convenient is a scheme such as this to our weak imaginations! It puts a comfortable cushion between the Creator's action and the action of his creature. God makes the creature and lays down its active capacity. Whatever happens whales will not fly nor eagles dive. But when whales dive and eagles fly, the action is their own. They need an attraction, a motive in face of which to act, but the action is theirs. Pious clauses can be added, to the effect that the action of the creature conforms to the divine will; but such qualifications leave our imaginations fundamentally undisturbed. The comfortable barrier between creative act and creaturely activity remains.

Now compare with that scholastic picture the physical doctrine prevalent today. Something called energy is the physical ultimate. Unlike Aristotelian substance with its inherent capacities, energy is not something which may or may not act. Energy always acts with all its force; for it, to act is to exist. The only thing 'potential' about it is its ability or liability to change the mode or the direction of its action. Apart from this element of 'potency', energy could be simply identified with the action in which it acts; nor has it any present embodiment, or actuality, save in its present phase of action. For energy, not to act is not to be.

What happens, then, if we make a finite reality of this sort the direct object of a divine creative act? The comfortable cushion between creative action and creaturely action vanishes. If God creates energies he creates going activities. What he causes to be is their acting as they do. We cannot even say that he causes them to act, for it is by their action that they are they. The self-being of the creature seems to be annihilated. Its whole active existence is a simple *fiat* of the divine will.

'Come now' we may be tempted to say, 'it is not so bad as that, or anyhow it need not remain so beyond the first moment. God creates myriads of energies each active in a pure or simple state, and each with the capacity of modifying its action in engaging with that of others. This self-modification of action is the creaturely thing.' Here is a comforting hypothesis, would it but stand; alas, it will not. The notion of energies active in a pure or simple state prior to mutual engagement, is physical nonsense. All activity is mutual as between energies, and all activity thus mutually engaged changes and redistributes itself.

If God creates energies he creates energies-in-act, and if energies-in-act then energies in mutual engagement, and if energies in mutual engagement then energies in perpetual change. We cannot conceive God as instituting anything physical, unless he institutes a piece of cosmic hurly-burly in full career, and with all its kaleidoscopic detail.

'Even so' we may say, catching at a straw, 'may not he institute a specimen stretch of the cosmic free-for-all, and then somehow withdraw from it, so as henceforth not to appoint the action of nature, but rather to steer it?' Yet surely this is a very feeble hypothesis. It arises from our wanting equally to say two things; that finite energies have some sort of existential insufficiency which makes them dependent for their being on God's creative act; and that they are so far independent in their being and action, as to make them genuine creatures and something in themselves. It is surely a weak evasion to prevent a collision between our two propositions by a distinction of time: 'They *were* instituted by God, they *are* active of themselves.' If God is able so to 'withdraw' from the creatures he has made as to let them be themselves, the gist of the matter is, that he is able to institute active creatures and yet to let them be themselves; and if he can do it now, could not he do it from the first moment?

To enforce the point, let us accept the hypothesis we are criticising, and ask what would have happened if God, after instituting by direct *fiat* his specimen stretch of cosmic hurly-burly, had *not* withdrawn from it so as to throw it in some measure on itself. In that case would God have created anything, or not? If anything which was so simply the *fiat* of divine will had not enough self-being to go on being a creature, then it had not enough to start being a creature. It was simply God's diagram or God's dream, and he could not be thought to withdraw from it, or throw it on itself. If, on the other hand, it already qualified as a created self-existence, why should God withdraw from it to make it so?

The purpose of so fantastic a dialectic is to leave standing the inescapable paradox: to affirm Creative Will is to affirm a power which institutes an activity active of itself, and not a mere phase of the creative activity.

We are driven to repeat in connexion with creation the query we raised in connexion with natural providence: 'Is the special form of the problem the result of scientific discoveries (or, should we say, scientific hypotheses)? It may be that our scientists find energy a convenient ultimate, just as an earlier generation did billiard-ball atoms, and an earlier generation still Aristotelian substances. May not a later generation smile at us, and wonder at a naivety which took pragmatic concepts for ontological truths?' Well, no one perhaps can guarantee us against the smiles of posterity, except by promising a total oblivion for us and all our works. We, standing where we stand, can only do our best to judge whether the energy-concept is of purely empirical status or whether it has its roots in the nature of our physical experience. We ought not to rule out the possibility that the progress of experimental enquiry may have driven scientists into sound philosophical sense. To speak for ourselves, we cannot but judge on philosophical grounds that physical interference being the only method of physical enquiry, physical action is the only physical reality we can ever encounter; and that in consequence a statement of the physical in terms of action must be the most economical, and the least obstructive to an interpretation of the phenomena. We are forced to admit that we cannot describe physical realities simply as they are in themselves; but we still have no grounds, and it seems can have none, to suppose them something quite different from activities.

In some minds the tidiness of a metaphysical system awakens nothing but suspicion; surely, to dovetail so nicely together, the conclusions arising from different arguments must have been cooked. The metaphysician himself cannot feel quite so suspicious—if he did, he would not be that metaphysician. Whatever view my reader may take of the metaphysical concord I proceed now to unveil, to me it can but seem due, right, and confirmatory of my thoughts. I refer to the concord between an interpretation of creation which accepts current physical theory and the general account of religious belief which I have propounded. If we take energy as our first-created stuff, we have the same undisguised paradox between creaturely action and the divine action through or in it, as we meet at every other level.

At every level the palliations of paradox are the same, and we have already indicated them sufficiently. The formal or logical palliative is the doctrine of analogy, which shews us that we are bound to break down over the joint between infinite and finite action, unable as we are to do better than talk about infinite action as a sort of finite action. The dynamic or pragmatic palliative is an account of religious thought setting before us such a practical relation to the divine in and through the creaturely, as precludes our having anything to do with that same mysterious joint between the finite and the infinite action.

CHAPTER VI

REVELATION AND HISTORY

To philosophise in universal terms about everything called religion or religious belief is only possible at a level of the most vapid generality. If we want to combine solidity of treatment with any breadth of induction we must choose our topic carefully; for example, we may take the theology of nature. Jews, Mohammedans, Neoplatonists and Rational Deists have shared with Christians the assurance of a First Cause, and acknowledged in the world the expression of divine goodness; Pantheists of various shades have at least concurred with us in finding some unity of cause behind phenomenal multiplicity. But turn from the theology of nature to the theology of revelation, and the case is altered. One can say in a broad sense that every great religion gives some indication of the source from which saving knowledge is derived; with some it is innate reason, with others ecstasy, with these sacred history, with those a person of more than common stature. One can make an inventory of such spiritual evidences, one can scarcely make a common analysis of them, they are so utterly different. To bracket the alleged sources of religious truth is like bracketing the various sources of income. All gainful occupations come under the rubric; yet there is no science of breadwinning of which medicine, carpentry, farming and accountancy are branches; and neither is there a common doctrine of revelation.

I shall make no apology, then, for discussing revelation as Christians understand it. I shall endeavour nevertheless to handle it philosophically, not dogmatically.

We have been pursuing the theme of a divine activity with which our own activity engages; and we have traced its roots into the realm of nature, where it displays itself in the formation or fostering of natural kinds and of their instances. Among natural kinds is the human. But mankind, however natural as an animal fact, escapes into another dimension through reason, initiative, and the accumulation of a cultural deposit. What the historian paints on a wide canvas, and the biographer on a narrow, is not so much the product of natural forces as the use, development and cultivation of them.

This at least is characteristic of religion in general, that it sees divine power on both sides of the divide, spanning the two realms of wild nature and of civilised endeavour. At an elementary stage, the gods both foster the growth of crops or herds, and direct or assist the arts of husbandry and herdsmanship. At a more advanced level, divine justice relates the favours or severities of nature to the historical destinies of the tribe, while from the human side inspiring and chastening the people in their reaction to nature's pressures. With the development of individual awareness, men become concerned over the split in themselves between instinctive urges and chosen policies; they look to God for the harmony in themselves of nature and mind, since both factors find their place in his single creative purpose.

Divine purpose embraces the two levels; it does not confuse them. The God who acts naturally in nature acts humanly in mankind. So his action in mankind embodies a purpose to which men by their own action can adhere. The purpose is everywhere; every man at every moment has his calling. It is *revealed* (so Christians hold) in certain typical, decisive and evident divine actions; these are revelation *par excellence*.

We can distinguish between the content and the mode of revelation. To discuss the content is simply to discuss Christian theology. We will confine out attention to the mode of it.

The Dean of York, Dr Alan Richardson, has argued in his recently published Bampton Lectures[1] that Revelation is just history with a special slant. He takes his stand against theologians

[1] History Sacred and Profane.

who say that the revealed and revealing story is not history at all, but something else for which the name of metahistory has been coined. For, they argue, it is not primarily about the actions of men, concerning which history treats; it is about the action of God, which is not a historical subject. The actions of men are open to examination by the common rules of evidence; the actions of God are proved by quite other criteria. The actions of men find expression in the literal sense of our language; the actions of God only in a transferred sense defying exact logical control. So say the metahistorians. The Dean of York finds their notion of metahistory both evasive and self-defeating. Evasive, as putting divine revelation beyond the reach of historical criticism; self-defeating, because by taking revelation out of our historical world it denies in effect that it has reached us. The word has failed after all to become flesh. No, says the Dean; revelation-history is sheer history.

There is certainly something at stake here, and something which calls for philosophical treatment. The issue is not purely philosophical; the theologian will have something to say on the conformity of the one doctrine or the other to the mind of scripture, or its adequacy to the saving effects of revelation. But theology will be liable to fight a blindfold battle unless the terms of dispute are philosophically clarified.

The Dean supports his thesis that revelation-history is just history by an appeal to admissions commonly made about the historical art itself. Historians who know their trade pretend to no such thing as a purely factual or objective history-writing. Interpretative concepts and schematic systematisations have to be employed; and they are never simply called for by the recorded evidence, nor simply verifiable from it. Why then, asks the Dean, may not the interpretative concepts of theology hold their place alongside of others? 'The history of God's dealings with Israel' need be no less historical, no more metahistorical, than 'the history of democratic development in England' or 'the rise and decline of free capitalism in the West'. For 'free capitalism' and 'English democracy' are no more to be accounted simple phenomena or simple groups of phenomena than is 'Israel's covenant-relationship with God'.

I hope I do not misrepresent the Dean in thus summarising the gist of his contention. If we are to estimate the force of it we shall need to remind ourselves a little more fully of the status of interpretative machinery in history-writing.

History, to be worthy of the name, involves some breadth of survey and some complexity of correlated facts. National history is typical history; and a nation is a multitude. A complete national history over any period might seem to involve the biographies of all the citizens who flourished in it. But supposing we had achieved the impossible and written all these biographies one by one, we should still have the history of the period to write. For history is an account of the way things went in general, through the mutual play of all these lives on one another, both moulding and moulded by traditions or institutions, both reactive to and creative of economic conditions. Biography is, in a sense, prior to history, if the biography is pure. But biography may itself be historical and presuppose the history it focusses. A political biography will handle its subject as a crossing of threads in the great web of historical complexity.

In a pure biography we may make it our ideal to show our hero's life as it appeared to himself, or perhaps to his neighbours. Our own attitudes and ideas are bound to colour the picture, but our aim will be to reduce their influence as far as is compatible with a lively rendering of the subject to our contemporaries. In history proper such an aim would be self-defeating. We can make no significant or unified story without importing diagrammatic concepts, 'creatures of the mind' such as economic balance, constitutional development and a host of others. And in the selection of these concepts we shall be governed by the views of our own time, its values and its problems, not simply by those of the times we undertake to describe. For example, we shall write the economic history of the Greek cities, or of the Roman Empire, though we are perfectly aware that no one is the classical age of either Rome or Greece understood public events in economic terms. But we know that our own materially complex civilisation must conjure with economic factors, or perish; and we are fascinated to observe how people in other ages dealt with analogous issues, however little they understood them.

To see what sort of analogy historical work offers for the sacred records of revelation, we have first to consider whether history proper or biography is the relevant model. On the face of it the heart of the Christian revelation looks like a task for the biographer; and the wellknown theological commonplace, that a biography of Christ cannot be written, will not settle the question in the opposite sense. If the personal destiny, the sayings and the sanctity of a historical person are proposed as the divine exemplar of every human life, it would seem that the material presented must be biographical material, whether or not we are in a position to organise it as we would the biography of a nineteenth-century divine. We cannot write up the biography of Christ *selon les règles,* but neither can we the biography of Socrates.

However that may be, it is plain that a biographical reading of the gospel material cannot be equivalent to a reading of it as divine revelation. The biographer as such concerns himself with his hero's intention in his acts, or meaning in his utterances. If his hero set any particular value on his person, action or destiny, say by relating them to the person or action of God, the biographer will do his best to convey it to us. So to understand the gospels biographically may be to determine what Christ thought about Christ; it is not to determine what we should think about him. To write Aristotle's biography is not in itself a commendation of Aristotelism, and biographies of Christ have been attempted which were anything but commendations of Christianity. A believing Christian may well feel that, could we but achieve it, an adequate and unbiassed presentation of Christ's mere biography would suffice to persuade a candid mind to think with Christ. Practically speaking there may be much to be said for this view. Instead of encumbering the gospel with readymade theology, try presenting it as biographically as possible and see if your hearer or reader will not do the necessary theologising for himself. Very well; but the point is pastoral, not philosophical. The theologising has still to be done, if Christ's life is to be taken as God's action. Theological interpretation is not reduced to biography either by being left to the reader's wit or by being prefigured in the hero's thoughts. As with theology, so with any science or doctrine. In studying or writing Sir Isaac Newton's biography we might become convinced by his ideas. But it would be as physicists, not as biographers, that we should be so convinced.

The Dean of York would I am sure agree with us. Whether the theological interpretation is made by us, or by the Church Fathers, by the Apostles or by Christ himself, it is not biography. No indeed; but may not it be history? Christ's own thoughts about his person and his mission related them to the total destiny of the human race and more narrowly to the history of the people of God; and his disciples' development of his ideas has by no means lessened their scope. Just as the historical significance of Napoleon Bonaparte or of Charles de Gaulle spreads a web of diagrammatic references over the human field past, present and to come, so does the theological significance of Christ. The choice and employment of diagrammatic concepts, and the detailed judgments resulting from their application all over the area, are grounded (as we said above) in our sense of our own predicament; you can call them functions of existential decision, if that sort of language gives you any joy. But if so much is true of history in general, it is more emphatically true of sacred history. No one affirms what Christians affirm about Christ without committing his own existence.

Does it follow from these premises that theological interpretation is historical interpretation? It does not. If history could be adequately defined as an interpretation of past events with the aid of diagrammatic fictions related to existential decision, then the theology of revelation could be proved to be history by being brought within the four corners of the definition. But if the definition is inadequate; if, to be history, an interpretation of the past requires further characteristics which the theology of revelation cannot claim; then it is not history. Here is an animal which shares with the horse every mammalian characteristic. Is it therefore a horse? Not unless it can show certain further distinguishing marks.

The historical characteristic which the theology of revelation fails to exhibit may be brought out by taking an example. After a desultory course of reading through ancient and patristic authors I pick up St Augustine's Confessions. The sudden change of climate astounds me. His predecessors belong to another world; my own soul speaks to me in St Augustine. In this man, I tell myself, a new humanity is born; we have been living him out ever since.

I have made a somewhat emotional remark; you will perhaps allow it some indulgence as the expression of immediate feeling, and let it go at that. But suppose you are so ill-advised as to take me up on it, and ask me to explain myself. And suppose that I, in my exalted mood, declare that St Augustine remains the inner soul of western man and that none of us can be ourselves otherwise than by evoking in ourselves the present action of that glorious saint. Would you agree that I was just talking history, only going, perhaps, a little deeper than historians commonly go? You would not. You would insist that historical connexions must run through historical channels.

But for my foolish and subsequent comment, my original remark, though highly coloured, might have passed with you as capable of an historical construction. Say that cultural and spiritual forces which have since remained effective were piling up in St Augustine's time and that he was the first notable figure to respond to them. Say that his writings became, after the Bible, the principal reading of Western Christendom and that our Reformers were as Augustinian as their Catholic opponents, so that the traditions and institutions which have shaped us all retain the imprint. Statements of this sort, whether true or false, are historical claims; and why? Because they relate my mind to St Augustine's by historical links; by books copied and read, by sermons preached and heard, by institutions built up and lived in. But once allow the Saint to jump the rails of historic sequence, to slip behind the scenes of time, and from some other dimension, as it were through the curtains of eternity, to put out an arm and touch us; then we are clean outside history. What is not history may still be true; it is a possible thought anyhow to some Christians that St Augustine from the heaven of his beatitude should potently act on our contemporaries; but it is not the supposition of an historical causality.

History spans the flux of events and the succession of generations with seeming continuities, like 'the Augustinian Spirit' or 'the Western democratic tradition', 'the English Monarchy' or 'the American people'. But history knows that these are not deathless entities; they are what we have called them, diagrammatic fictions. History also knows to what sorts of realities these fictions have to be referred; that is, to individual human actions, their mutual influences and mass effects.

It follows from the strokes we have added to the definition of history that the story which constitutes revelation is not just history of a rather deep sort. Theological history does not and cannot resolve its mythical diagrams into the succession or interplay of human acts; they must stand for a reality which is the continuous operation of a divine will. Whatever believers may think about St Augustine, they unquestionably hold that God is an historical agent not pinned to a point of time, but able as out of another dimension to exert his power at every moment; and if sacred history does not show the hand of God it neither is nor mediates divine revelation.

If, then, sacred history is not just a rather deep sort of history, is it metahistory? But what on earth is metahistory? We know what history is, for we know what historians do. But metahistorians? Are there any such animals? The name appears to be proposed as a cant term for sacred historians. But if so, we are not much enlightened by being told that this is what they are. Or is the name valued for its analogical suggestiveness? I suppose it is. But it is hard to see how the analogy applies. We may begin by setting aside the purely pedantic point that the very name 'Metaphysics' arises from the misunderstanding of a title in the Aristotelian corpus. For in fact the term has been taken to mean 'Advanced Physics' or 'Super-Physics', it being always understood that 'physics' in this connexion does not mean the science tied to what we call physical method, but study in the nature (*physis*) of things: Metaphysics has been thought to be a more deep, or more abstract, study of the nature of real beings than the positive sciences attempt; a study which employs logical or philosophical rather than empirical instruments, and which interprets the bearing of merely physical doctrines in some profound or ultimate way.

Our contemporaries, disgusted with metaphysics as so conceived, have nevertheless borrowed the analogy and talked about *metalogic*. There are the ground-level logical systems which interpret the structures of rational discourse; but it is possible to take a higher level and examine the structure essential to any logic as such. We can call this higher level *metalogic* if we like.

Now what I wish to remark is that metalogic and metaphysic (as formerly conceived) have two characteristics in common. First, *meta-* can in both cases be interpreted as 'higher-level' and be directly attached to the name it prefixes. Metaphysics was higher-level 'physics', a sort of super-nature-study; metalogic is higher-level logic. Then second, each arises from a critique, or interpretation, of its subject-science. The difficulty of realising this two-sided model in the field of history is manifest. There is a philosophical criteriology of history, but it is not itself a super-history, for it is not a story of any kind; and neither is it a theology. Revelation-history is indeed a sort of history, or anyhow a kind of story; but what sense can we give to *meta-* in connexion with it? Is 'saving history', though history, a highly abstract or general pattern of events in which the happenings of everyday history find their place? To all evidence it is not; it is rather that, in highly particular historical events, God from time to time shows his hand with a plainness the enlightened eye cannot mistake.

Or is metahistory, without being more general or abstract, an altogether other-level story: a story of God's doings behind a story of man's? In Homer's poem, the comedy of Olympus stands behind the tragedy of Ilium; we can distinguish the history of Apollo or Athena from the contemporaneous fortunes of Hector or Agamemnon. No doubt; but that is unreflective paganism. To put a story behind a story is not only heathen error but senseless duplication. God has no history; what is done in history through the action of his will is done by, and happens to his creatures. There is a story of how Shakespeare comes to write his drama and there is a story of how the actors set about to put it on the stage. The Author of Being goes through no labours of composition and there is no prior history of his thoughts. The only history we have is of what he does in and through his creatures, if only we can see the pattern, or grasp the whole.

If this is what the Dean contends for when he protests that sacred history is history, not metahistory, he is contending for a vital truth. Though the history of God's action is the history of God's action, and not simply of men's, yet the form his historical action takes is exhausted by what he causes his creatures, rational or irrational, animate or inanimate, to do. The word 'history' is of course notoriously ambiguous; it is used objectively of the event-series, and subjectively of a human science or pursuit. Taking the objective sense, we may say that everything God does in the human sphere is human history; taking history as the name of a human science, we shall say that it treats of the things God does, but not of his doing them. We shall add that God does much in human life of which history does not treat; for not being of public concern, it falls through the historian's net.

The Dean of York's analogy between histories sacred and profane requires that the diagrammatic or mythical fictions employed by the sacred science should run parallel to those used by the secular; that is to say, that they should diagrammatise intelligible continuities in the successive acts and destinies of creatures. Where (let us say) the historian sees a continuity of

economic logic, the theologian sees a continuity of divine purpose. The historian uses economic fictions to express what he
has to say; the theologian uses a mythology of manlike projects
in a divine mind. The parallel is in so far incomplete, that the
historian's rational continuities fall within the field of earthly
history, even if they are headed towards utopian dreams; whereas
the continuities of purpose acknowledged by the theologian
run towards goals beyond the world we know. But we must
not exaggerate the difference—the future state conventionally
called 'heaven' is taken to be a future state of God's creatures;
so that the threads of purpose finished off and knotted there do
not for that reason run beyond all creaturely being or action.

Such is the bearing of mythical fictions which best squares
with the Dean of York's thesis; but they have another bearing
which the metahistorians will delight to emphasise. Mythic
symbols do not only express the purpose of God's historic action,
they also give expression to the fact that it is God who acts.
This element in the mythic story is not human history, whatever
it is; and if anyone likes to call it metahistory, I suppose he is
welcome to do so. We see an example, when the unique action
and personal presence of the divine in Jesus is called a 'coming
down from heaven'. Such language does not stand alone; how
often does God visit his people in the Old Testament, or in their
perversity withdraw his presence! If we gave our imagination
rein, it might present us with an almost Homeric picture of
celestial comings and goings.

What are we to say of such language? Surely that its value is
found in its most general effect; it keeps us in mind throughout
the story that the Author of it is no earthly being. It can scarcely
be said to find a place in the substance of what is revealed; here
we must take sides with the Dean of York. The revelation
is what God does in the history, could we but see the drift
of it.

And yet—and yet—how difficult these matters are to talk
about, and what a host of qualifications one finds oneself driven
to introduce! The position we have laid down might suggest

that the history of mankind, or perhaps of God's people, could we but read it rightly, would show the working of a continuous and tranquil providence, leading God's creatures to their perfection; much as we might hope to see the superficially disconnected passages composing a certain sort of novel or play fall into a continuous march of meaning. But the God of revelation, unlike the storyteller or playwright, continually interrupts his own composition and talks to his characters; not that his interventions are really interruptions, for it is through them that he steers the characters and makes the plot. Sacred history is primarily concerned with the actions and fortunes of people in dialogue with God; natural events serving providential ends, and ungodly men forwarding purposes which are nothing to them, play a part, but an altogether subsidiary part. And so, to an eye cast back over the tract of sacred history, the mythic picture of a traffic between heaven and earth easily reinstates itself. Sacred history is seen not as what God does on earth, but as God's omnipotent utterances from heaven, and their consequences in human obedience or defiance.

But God's speaking from heaven is a myth. God revealed himself in former times, as he does now, by things done on earth. If we read a self-disclosure of God to us in the sacred history behind us, we must surely allow that the characters in the story we look back upon read the will of God in the history which lay behind them or about them. What looks to us from the distance like a smooth swift current running up to throw a breaker on our shore, is seen on a closer view to ruck itself in wave after wave; the history which gathers itself into a head to thunder in our ears so gathered itself and so spoke for those people of old time whose successive responses to the voice are now the history that speaks to us.

What Isaiah did in obedience to the God of history would in due course become part of the revealing story; in the moment of his obedience he would not see it in such colours, but simply as the thing he was called to do. We, reading in Isaiah's action the action of God, may raise the speculative question of the causal

97

relation between the divine will and the human; it was no question to Isaiah and it is of no practical bearing on us, who have only to act in face of the divine will disclosed.

When we used the figure we just now found convenient, of water gathering in a wave to thunder its message in our ears, the artificiality was evident; there is no articulate voice in breaking waves, unless our imagination lends it to them. We need not be so wantonly fanciful, to hear a message in the movement of history. We may say that the events speak for themselves. But in sober exactitude, we cannot admit it; to gather the lesson of facts is always the work of the mind. Not, however, that the mental work need be voluntary, that questions need be painfully posed and answers found. The interpretation may be both involuntary and immediate. In straightforward cases the experience is familiar. A Christian confronted with the roadside spectacle which halted the Good Samaritan does not have to ask himself what God requires of him.

When we try to appreciate the experience of men receiving (as they deem) divine communication, we find ourselves time and again in doubt where to put the point of punctuation between the divine and the human. Must there not be a divine datum of some kind, whether a fact presented or a word revealed, and then following upon it an activity of the human agent, pondering, interpreting, inferring, obeying? But if so, where does the divine end and the human begin? And what is the nature of the mysterious datum?

It is the general purpose of our argument to show that the question of this point of punctuation, as a speculative question, does not arise. The whole drift of events around us, in us and through us, is (we must believe) carried by the divine will, though mostly it is dark to us. If any part of it is made luminous there is the datum. If we can talk of a point of punctuation, it is not a point between the divine and the creaturely but between the revealing and the reactive. At any given moment a man will be called upon to make some voluntary reaction. Because it is what he is called to do, he must view it as his own. Anything preceding it may be taken as signifying the divine will which calls for it.

The point of punctuation between the revealing and the reactive moves forwards or backwards as the spotlight of voluntary decision moves. Let us suppose that Isaiah sees the Assyrian armies marching on Palestine and feels called to ask himself the prophet's question: What is the purpose of God in willing or suffering such things to come to pass? While he is in such a posture, the divine datum is the military fact; the activity to which Isaiah is called is to ask his question. But then things need not go like this. The purpose of God in the Assyrian movement may be blindingly clear from the first—Assyria is the scourge in the hand of God's indignation. Then the point of punctuation moves; the divine purpose is the datum; Isaiah's calling is to proclaim it. But it may not go like this either. The message (we may suppose) is so compulsive, the seer cannot do otherwise than prophesy; it is all one to see the truth and to proclaim it; the hand of the Lord is upon him, to carry him into the temple-court, and to pour the words from his lips. Then all of this is datum, all is divine act. The moment of decision, the challenge to the prophet's will, may not come until the flow of his eloquence is interrupted. The princes seize him for spreading alarm and despondency in time of crisis. How now is he to behave?

There is only one practical relation of the human person to the divine, and that is the voluntary relation of which faith, obedience, love and their contraries are the modalities. That is why the point of punctuation we have been marking is the only genuine point of punctuation. There are other supposed points, but since they are illusory, the attempt to place them leads to nothing but bewilderment.

For example, there is the psychological point and there is the epistemological point. The psychological point is supposed to come between some experience of a type uniquely revelatory, and supervenient experiences appropriating it or developing it. The placing of the epistemological point is to follow somewhat similar principles—only the approach is different. Instead of looking for a psychical event in which it can be supposed that God uniquely affects the human spirit, we look for an object of awareness set pure before the mind, prior to all the doubtless fallible processes of mental interpretation.

Neither line of approach can lead to anything but a mare's nest. All that needs to be said about the psychological approach is that there is no sort of experience which must be revelatory and no sort of experience that may not be. As to the epistemological quest, we remark at once that it is conceived by analogy with the quest for pure sense data in the field of sensory perception. But a sound philosophy removes the basis of the analogy. For either there are no sense data, or if there are any they have no objective status but are simply the first conscious reactions of a nervous system engaged by the action of forces exterior or interior to our bodies. No doubt our physical experience starts from sensory reports of which we have to suppose or find the meaning. Our experience of the divine has no such starting-point; it begins with a mental recognition, however immediate, however elementary, of a superhuman action in that same creaturely existence which sense forces upon our attention.

The motive behind the psychological quest is the unwelcome suspicion that we dream up all our religion for ourselves and are nowhere subject to a supernatural touch. The motive of the epistemological quest is the desire to strip down all human colouring, all biassed interpretations of the divine and reach a hard datum. The psychological quest is more concerned with the question 'Can and does revelation occur?', the epistemological with the question, 'How are we to winnow the grain from the chaff?' But the two quests easily fuse. Perhaps Rudolf Otto's *Das Heilige* succumbed to both attractions. I do not mean that the path he followed led him to nothing better than a confusion between two mares' nests. The descriptive part of his work is of outstanding merit. Any pedant can correct his philosophy; it took genius to disclose what he disclosed.

For simplicity's sake we may lump the two conceptions together under the name of pure-datum theory. Pure-datum theory in all sorts of forms and applications was rife in the Age of Reason, as students of philosophical history will scarcely need to be reminded. Social theorists used to search for a pure reign of natural law obtaining before the questionable artificiality of political life obscured it. They no longer do, and let us hope that theologians will soon stop hunting for a pure datum of revelation prior to those necessary evils, reflection and communication. The datum for any mind is an involuntary thought; before we reflect, something has struck us. But involuntary thought is not specially free from admixtures of the all-too-human.

Pure-datum theory is an attempt to reconcile two propositions: first that God reveals himself authoritatively; and second that formulations of the revealed truth which reach us are subject to testing, criticism and revision. The motive becomes clear when, in *Our Experience of God*, my friend Professor H. D. Lewis takes me to task for removing the punctuation-mark between divine revelation and human reflection upon it. If, he says, we extend the revealing work of God into the process of reflection, we shall canonise as simply divine everything Apostles or Church Fathers, not to name lesser or later authorities, have said or written.

In saying this, the Professor makes the charitable supposition that I am a Christian, with a faith in ascertainably revealed truth. But for his charity, the Professor might equally well tie the antithesis to my tail. If I remove the punctuation-mark between revelation and reflection, and if I expose the reflection to criticism, everything goes into the melting-pot; I am left with no revelation at all.

Pair the thesis with the antithesis, and you present me with a classical dilemma. If I concede criticism its rights I have no revealed data; if I maintain revealed data, I muzzle criticism. So either criticism is out of court, or there are no revealed data.

What are we to do with the dilemma? We will universalise it. The paradox it builds upon is typical of the theologian's predicament all over the field of his concern; and the evasion of paradox by a distinction of time is no less typical of the apologist's temptations. The paradox is, that God authoritatively reveals himself through fallible thoughts; and the solution by temporal distinction is that he first reveals himself to thought, but that the thought, thinking itself out, become fallible. Even if the solution sounded theoretically convincing it would remain practically useless. There is no means of fixing the point at which apostolic or other thoughts begin thinking themselves out. Practically speaking, we lose nothing by swallowing the paradox. God reveals himself effectively through fallible minds and takes care that their imperfections shall not frustrate his purpose; for through his continued operation in us he winnows out in us the wheat from the chaff.

Whatever theories we choose to put up, we have no practical alternative—we have simply to let the winnowing proceed. That is, we shall rethink ancient thoughts, removing irrelevance and correcting bias; we shall not dig for thoughtless data. Everyone does the winnowing, even the simplest bible-Christians. A naive anachronism and an unconscious selectivity often achieve more than strenuous critical effort. Your theologian first defines himself back into the First Century by exegetical precision, and then argues himself out of it again through existential agonies. There is much to be said here as elsewhere for taking things easy, and doing what comes naturally.

I will conclude the chapter by putting together the account of divine revelation to which our discussion has pointed. It will be opportune to recall first what it is that we are defining. We are attempting to show how an orthodox Christian must think on the subject, if he is to think sense. We are not attempting to show why anyone should be an orthodox Christian.

We lay down, then, as the general context of the doctrine the belief that God's will takes effect in his creatures' action or destiny, so that there is always a Will to be embraced, could we but perceive its drift. Within this context we distinguish by two characteristics the events constituting revelation in the special sense. First, they are involved in an activity of God for the eternal salvation of his rational creatures. Second, they are events in which the relation of human instrument to divine act becomes transparent; that is to say, that at vital points human intention is brought into such an accord with divine intention that men effectively know and intelligibly proclaim what God does in them or before their eyes.

It is enough, that the saving action should become effectively known. There are imperfections in the media of revelation, but the Christian who supposes himself to be effectively enlightened believes *ipso facto* that they have not defeated the divine intention. So long as the saving purpose triumphs, the acknowledgement and display of human fallibilities can take nothing from the perfection of the divine work; divine power being as much shown in overcoming the weakness of its instruments, as it is shown in shaping them to its purpose. The paradigm is Christ's ability to play his part, with a mental furniture acquired from his village rabbi. For who can think that his mission would have been more gloriously performed with instruments other than these?

I hope these remarks have not sounded too pious for their occasion. But it is really useless to pretend that a theory of revelation is what it purports to be, unless it will accommodate the statement of a positive faith.

CHAPTER VII

THE THEOLOGY OF WILL

IT is no part of our purpose to prescribe an exclusively religious approach to theistic belief. We do not deny of the general character of the universe at any level, that it is indicative of God. Only we argue that God, however and wherever indicated, must be understood as a being about whom we have something to do. We have taken this consideration as decisive for the way we should conceive the relation of creatures to God at any point; it can scarcely be less decisive for the way in which we must conceive of God himself.

How, then, are we to conceive of God? It may provide a useful opening to the question if we examine the relation between two principles; principles which we have several times presented side-by-side as palliatives of paradox. The paradox was always the same paradox; we ran our heads against it sooner or later, whether we were discussing the theology of nature, of revelation, or of grace. It was the paradox of two agents for an identical action, the one creaturely, the other divine; and we offered two palliatives, the one logical, the other pragmatic.

Our logical palliative was that mossy piece of scholastic lore, 'analogical predication'; the doctrine that what is said of God and of creatures is said of the two subjects in an analogous, not an identical, sense. Two agents for the same act would be indeed impossible, were they both agents in the same sense and on the same level. The clearest example is offered by the theology of Grace. If God were a voluntary agent just as I am a voluntary agent, my good deed could not be his work, for it is my action. The head-on collision of incompatible assertions does not in fact take place; it is true that I am unequipped to think of God's agency otherwise than in terms of my own; it is false that I believe it to be of the same sort.

So much for the logical palliative. The pragmatic lay in the line of practical concern with God. The believer refers his conduct to divine purpose expressed or expressible in creaturely events. He does not and cannot relate it to any supposed point at which an underlying act of the divine power initiates or bears upon creaturely action. All he can practically do is take for granted the relation of creaturely action to its divine 'cause'; and so it is the less scandalous that he cannot resolve the paradox involved in that relation.

Such were our two palliatives. If we set the two before us and compare them, it must strike us immediately that where the first is general in its effect, the second is discriminatory. The doctrine of analogical predication lays it down that *whatever* is said about God must be stated in improper terms and be liable to a sort of logical discount. The pragmatic consideration discriminates between a cloudy, paradoxical realm of metaphysical relation which in the nature of the case we cannot explore, and a realm of divine purpose which constitutes our vital field of concern. If the realm offered us were as obscure as the realm denied to us, there would be little consolation in such a discrimination. But, on the contrary, the suggestion made to us is that, being directly concerned with divine will in the form of purpose, we must, can, and do sufficiently understand it.

The difference we have noted in the scope of our two palliative principles does not set them at variance; it fits them to supplement one another. The doctine of analogical predication, taken by itself, is too open and undefined to serve as a justification for any statement. Some analogical statements may be meaningful, others stretch analogy so far as to be vapid or self-contradictory. We want to know that the analogical propositions on which we build our theology are substantial and tolerably consistent. It is here that our pragmatic palliative promises to help us. For it distinguishes between areas of discourse bearing upon theology which, if both analogical, are not equally unmanageable.

It may not offer us the choice of building on sand or of building on granite; it can perhaps offer us a choice between loose sand and settled clay. Out first business should be to make sure of our foundations. Even if we aspire to read the riddle of dynamic relation between creative and creaturely act, we may not be well-advised to approach it direct. We may be wiser if we hope to clarify it inferentially by first attending to what we can more distinctly conceive.

The clarity with which we are to begin is tied to pragmatic concern, and we may usefully start by putting our finger on the tie. The divine will with which we have to do must be a divine will which we can see ourselves doing; there must be a formal identity between what I understand God to intend for me and what I embrace as his intention and so perform. His will must be taken by me as a blue-print (so to speak) for voluntary action on the part of such a being as myself. The point, be it understood, is a logical point. It says nothing to the success or ill-success of men in grasping the particular will of God. Perhaps our appreciation of the divine purpose is never free from serious distortion. It remains that if the distortion could be corrected the true statement resulting would lay down a possible project for active human adoption; and that the distorted version is itself such a project.

In view of so logical a conclusion, ought we to infer that we were wrong in accepting the claim of analogical predication to cover all statements about God? Have we not here statements about God's intentions for us, which are not analogical at all, but perfectly literal? The answer to this question is not simple. We must distinguish. No element of theological analogy is involved in the statement of what God intends, when he intends what I should do; but analogy is involved in the statement that God intends it. God's act of intending is not identical with my act of intending, how could it be? The whole mode of divine being and action is other than the human. So in the whole statement 'God wills that . . .' analogy is involved; but attention will commonly be focussed on the part of the statement which does not involve it—the part which expresses what we have to do.

It is a laudable desire to edge analogy clean out of the picture if we can; every decent thinker must pursue clarity with all his might. We may hope to advance the good cause by suggesting that when God wills for me to will, he not only wills a project suitable for my willing, he adopts in so doing my way of willing it. For if so, a human account may be literally true not only of what God wills, but of his willing. Yes, but though we seem to have cleared the centre of our mental field, we cannot stop analogy from lurking in the margin. To say that God adopts our volitional mode is to place him outside our sphere, and to attribute to him an act (of 'adopting') which cannot be understood literally. To strip away the last rag of analogy, we must say that God simply does will as his creatures will. And that is to make his action and their action merely identical; it is to embrace that vacuous form of pantheism, which adds nothing to naturalism save an ill-justified emotional aura. The point hardly needs pressing. One who did not need to adopt the person of Hamlet could be no other than the Prince of Denmark. If an actor *adopts* the character, then *ex vi termini* he is not Hamlet, nor is his act of adopting the Hamlet-persona a Hamlet-action. Never mind, it is still a human action, and as such perfectly intelligible to us. Whereas if God adopts the human mode, his action in so doing is not human action, and our inevitably human manner of conceiving it is a typical piece of theological analogy.

We digress—we have made it our present business to exploit clarity, not to hunt analogy. We have put our finger, as we said, on the pragmatic point in which clarity centres. Can we spread at all the light that radiates from there? One might think not. Is not the case in which divine will prescribes my duty or adumbrates my hope a quite special case? How are we to speak of the intentions which that will forms in natural events? What God wills for my virtue or my happiness, I am bound to conceive. What he designs through the events of nature, how shall I even guess?

Nevertheless, we must not let so promising a clue go out of our hands without a struggle. We may begin by attacking the hard line which has just been drawn round the privileged case, cutting it out of its context. The divine will that is clear for me is the will prescribing an action so immediate and so particular that I can set about it; yet the divine purpose in thus prescribing extends more widely—extends, indeed, almost to infinity. Every 'good work that God has prepared for us to walk in' will be believed by us to find its place in vaster schemes and to serve remoter purposes, faintly conjectured by us at the best; purposes which the Christian hope carries beyond the confines of this present world.

Bearing in mind the distinction we have just drawn between the focus of clarity and the penumbra which surrounds it, let us turn back to the alleged mystery of God's intention in the realm of natural process. What is mysterious here? God's immediate intention in the natural event we are considering, or the penumbra—his wider and ulterior aim? Surely it is the latter. The immediate and particular will of the Creator is that each created energy should act according to its kind. That is the meaning of saying that the Creator wills the existence of such a being, for such a being can exist only by exercising such an action; he cannot will the existence without willing the activity. If there is any mystery here about what God wills, the mystery is natural, not theological; it is the mystery which shrouds the being or action of physical ultimates. We cannot determine the immediate divine will for atomic (or as we now somewhat absurdly say, sub-atomic) energies, because we cannot perfectly isolate or define those energies themselves. If we could know them as they are, we should know what their Creator immediately wills in them.

We find in fact that we talk and speculate about physical ultimates, not about God's immediate will in them; for we recognise that the second consideration adds nothing to the first. *That* God wills the several processes of nature is a matter of awe and of amazement; *what* he wills for them raises no question beyond the scientific. But elementary energies and their actions do not strike us as providing a sufficient object of the creative intention; and we wonder freely enough about God's ulterior purposes in relation to them. What complex pattern do they help to build? Towards what nobler creatures do they pave the road?

Here indeed are mysteries; not impenetrable mysteries, however, nor mysteries which embody much theological analogy in their composition. We may be baffled in reflecting upon them by ignorance of essential facts; we do not suffer any great difficulty in stating what it is we want to know. Natural discovery assures us that elementary agents enter into larger complexes; so when we ask what complexes of the kind the Creator of elementary systems has in view, we know what we are talking about. Evolutionary developments lead to nobler creatures, through transitions of which we have some comprehension; so if we let ourselves wonder what further evolutionary designs are in the will of God, we are not carried into any metaphysical depths. Nor do we suppose that any wider complexes or nobler creatures that may result will call for new thoughts about the relation of creatures to their Creator. All such developments, we take it, will consist of real finite processes, creatures of God as others are.

There is one very general puzzle which troubles our imaginations when we explore natural Providence—the appearance of a conflict between the immediate and the ulterior purposes of God. The immediate purpose is that each created energy should be itself in its place and act according to its kind. But surely it would serve the ultimate purpose more smoothly if it were free to act in more direct obedience to that purpose and with less restriction to the limits of its native character. Why should there be constant setbacks and age-long delays to larger purpose from the recalcitrance of the very agents created for its realisation? If God arranges things thus, then truly his thoughts are not as our thoughts, and creative purpose can be called purpose at all only by a wide stretch of analogy.

Such is the suggestion which readily presents itself to our minds. Yet we do not find ourselves invoking the negative implications of the analogical principle when we proceed to an analysis of the problem. What we require is not a stretched conception of 'purpose' but a proper understanding of nature. It belongs to the nature of a world such as this (and we can conceive no other) that it should consist of self-acting parts. God will not set his heart on the streamlining of a plan, but on the realisation of a world. It is a foolish teacher who values a standard level or a preconceived pattern of school activities otherwise than as supplying a form in which his pupils may realise themselves. Who could attribute to God such doctrinaire folly? We may speak of the inexhaustible patience of God in achieving his wider aims. We cannot seriously suppose it to be a patience which has any impatience to overcome or any disappointment to discount; for that would be to accuse him of not knowing the sort of world he designs to make.

The furthest stretch of the divine patience seems to manifest itself in the human sphere: our Creator tolerates our perversity. We have the ability to overrule our mere nature in the interest of larger purposes; yet we abuse that ability, or fail to use it. A voluntary agent such as we are is indeed both an element in larger purposes and himself a microcosm of elements to be ordered. In either capacity he may fail, and as well by perversity of choice as by natural limitation. Yet, valuing as we do our freedom above all things, we are under no special difficulty in seeing why our Creator should support it; we can well conceive that he should will no fulfilment of human good otherwise than by attracting men's free decisions. What we cannot conceive is the causal joint (as it were) between omnipotent creativity and free creaturehood. But that is the very problem which we have reserved all along, and for which analogical justification must be so heavily invoked. How God works in creating, that is the mystery; not the purposes his working achieves.

We conclude in general that divine purpose in the world is a notion fundamentally clear. The complexity, the scope, the ultimate goals of God's will must indeed baffle us; but so (in some measure) may the ulterior aims of our fellow-creatures, without becoming metaphysical mysteries to us on that account. Having settled the point to our present satisfaction, we proceed to take the next step. We were to try (were we not?) to develop an account of the Divine Being, which should stand in the closest possible relation to that aspect of his action which is both practically immediate and theoretically clear to us. And is it not evident without more ado that the God of commanding purpose is acknowledged as sovereign will? To carry the enquiry further can be only to ask what more is to be said about such a will.

God is will, and as such is an agency to which our own voluntary and intellectual being offers the sole analogy or clue. How, then, does the divine act differ from ours? God must be such that he can will for every sort of creature once it is created, and also will what created forms there shall be. Such a will can only be defined by its unrestricted freedom. It is not the will of a determinate being, operating within a certain charter of function or scope of effect. It is all that it does, and chooses to be all that it is.

No one can deny that such a description stretches analogy to a far point; but still it is not meaningless to us. It would presumably be so, if our own voluntary powers were fixed to a single level of performance, or a set range of concerns. They are not; we have some ability to liberate our purpose from the satisfying of set desires to the pursuit of adopted projects, or from the realisation of personal interests to the support of neighbourly aims. The ideal of a will with no given canoe to paddle, so far from being meaningless to us, defines the very goal of our aspiration. But here is a subject on which I have written more than enough elsewhere; and in spite of the importance of the topic, I will not go over old ground.

Perhaps indeed my readers will scarcely wish to question the appropriateness of a voluntarist account of the divine nature to a practical concern with divine purpose. They may be more inclined to wonder whether a theology with so pragmatic a basis will square with the requirements of metaphysical speculation; and on this head we feel obliged to satisfy them if we can. For while we have laid it down that no God can mean anything to us but a God about whom we have something to do, we have by no means wished to deny that the existence of such a God is indicated to us by a contemplation of finite being. What conception of God, then, naturally results from the time-honoured argument *a contingentia mundi?*

Here is old ground indeed, but so far from feeling a disinclination from treading over it, I have the strongest motive in the desire to stamp out the traces of my youthful errors. In a book called *Finite and Infinite* I compromised between voluntarism and formalism in a way which now seems to me to have been perverse; and I take the present opportunity to review the argument from finite existence to deity as that treatise handled it.

I have no wish to withdraw the whole basis of the argument. It was an argument about *being*, and I am no more prepared now that I was then to hear *being* made fun of. Our contemporaries say, and properly enough, that all talk of 'being' should be tied down to the senses of the verb *to be* which function in natural sentences. It does not concern us here to sort out all the uses there are, but to insist on the existential. The ancients were right when they said that the normal copulative use contains the existential sense. Such statements as 'Surds are unrealisable numbers' or 'Mermaids are fish-tailed girls' are manifest sophistications. The primary use of the so-called copula is that which states existence. There is no need to say 'Giraffes are the longest-necked mammals *and there are giraffes*'. The affirmation of existence does not require to be added; in the sophisticated usages it is understood to be subtracted. Copulatives are common, pure existentials are rare. But that is no evidence of the uncommonness of existential affirmation; it is an evidence that the naked issue of existence/non-existence is not of very frequent concern. When it crops up, it can be commonplace enough. 'There isn't any butter.'—'Oh yes there is; look on the middle shelf.'

If the ancients were in error, it was not in finding an affirmation of existence in the copula; it was in giving the verb *to be* a uniqueness of status which it cannot claim. The copula is used in sentences expressing quality or state or classification. Other verbs give direct expression to action; and the primary sense of such verbs contains an equally plain existential affirmation. Equally plain, or perhaps even plainer; the action-verb casts more light than the copulative *to be* on the nature of existential affirmation in general. 'If he threw half a brick at you, he was (there)' is as good an inference as 'If he was six foot tall, he was (there).' Both inferences are of the sort called immediate—the logical operation being simply the omission in the conclusion of much that was stated in the premise. Only his throwing half a brick is an actual phase of the activity wherein his existence lies, whereas his being six foot tall is an accidental relation between the area effectively occupied by the physical elements basic to him, and the arbitrarily fixed standard of a foot-rule.

When we say that our fellow-creatures, animate or inanimate, are . . ., we do not mean that they present phenomena which allow of a stated classification, or that they will respond to an implied test, or even that they interact with us in a certain way. These are consequences or signs of their being . . .; they actually are in and as the activity they exercise. And it is this that active verbs of which they are the subjects directly express. What such verbs do not commonly express is the systematic continuity of the action process, and so, of the subject's existence. Sentences containing the verb *to be* are more likely to take care of that aspect.

Descartes was perfectly correct, when he derived 'I am' from 'I think'. His error was to restrict the modalities of his existence to the phases of his thought; he was right in judging that his being, stripped of all modalities of action, would be an unrealisable abstraction. The true importance of his *cogito* was that it yielded him a *pure* existential statement; indeed, an indubitably pure one. By a pure existential I mean one in which a modality of action is directly attributed to the subject of that action. Most statements with existential content are impure, even when they contain verbs of action. 'The hammer drives the nail' suggests by its logical form that there is a hammer and that it does the driving. But I have no evidence of that, nor can I seriously believe it. There are physical reals such as to cohere in the mass which has the hammer-form, and which allows of being handled in a certain way, with the effect that . . . The impure existential apes the pure, just as statements about mermaids ape statements about fishes. We talk as though 'being a hammer' were a way for something to be. We shall not, let us hope, base metaphysical conclusions on such careless language. It is mere frivolity to philosophise the way we talk before we think, rather than the way we talk after we have reflected on all we have sound reason to believe.

The last few paragraphs I have written do little more than summarise what I expounded at length in my old book under the heading ESSE EST OPERARI. The formula was no more accurate than the Berkeleian PERCIPI to which it was a counterblast; but it may serve to epitomise our position no worse than Berkeley's epigram served to epitomise his. It can fairly be contested on the ground that the terms equated and not equivalent. ESSE may be said to abstract the focality of an agency from the fact and the mode of its activity. It will remain that the equated terms are logically inseparable. We can say UBI ESSE, IBI DATUR OPERATIO or OMNE ENS OPERATUR. Logically inseparable, not simply *de facto*. 'Where being is, there is activity' is not like 'Where there is smoke there is fire.'

It is beside our present purpose to refine on the point. Our concern is to examine the traditional theology of being which we re-erected on the basis of this doctrine. The theist (we claimed) is the man who does full justice to the question 'Why is it so?' as asked about any fact whatever of finite existence. Where the question is raised, everyone will no doubt look first for proximate and finite grounds of explanation. But when one has chased explanation back from position to position, and still finds himself in face of brute fact, one comes to realise that the state of the case will not be altered if he hunts the trail *ad infinitum*. Not only are any explanatory first facts we take, brute facts; the rule by which they determine (and so explain) subsequent facts is brute fact also. To say that fact remains brute fact, and to say that it continues to prompt the question why it is so, is to say one and the same thing.

I proceeded in my old book to analyse that stubborn question. If we can meaningfully ask why it is so, we must be distinguishing between an 'it' and a suchness or so-ness which might not but does characterise it. We cannot ask the question if the subject and predicate terms are synonymous. It is senseless to ask why a man (as such) is a man, or a living thing a living thing. And if anything whatsoever can give rise to the question, then all conceivably alternative suchnesses must fall on the predicate side. The 'it' whose having any given suchness is a brute fact can have no character itself but that of being actual. Then the question will run, 'Why should it, being an actuality, have the mode of actuality we find it to have?' The question would be merely verbal, were it not for two considerations: first, that we take activity to be the character basic to all existence we can meaningfully conceive; and second, that we conceive activity in general, and experience it in ourselves, as capable of varying its form, mode or suchness. It is perfectly natural, then, that confronted with any manifestation of (active) existence we should ask why it is what it is or does what it does. That, then, is the question to which we find no final answer within the natural world.

The paragraph I have just written is the mere epitome of a whole philosophy of being, to which I devoted the best part of my old book; and though there are statements and arguments there which I should now wish to rephrase, I stand by the position as a whole. So far, then, so good. But now we reach the crucial point. When we ask 'Why is it so?' what sort of explanation do we seek? If the attachment of the modality to the existential act appears arbitrary or unexplained, then what attachment of the one to the other would satisfy us? Why do not we say (as atheists are content to say) that brute fact is the inevitable character of such an attachment?

I can think of two answers, the formalist and the voluntarist. In my old book I gave the formalist answer. If 'it' puzzles us by being 'so' rather than otherwise, it is because we contrast it with an 'it' that should stand above and be exempt from such arbitrary determinations; that is, an active existence or existent activity which should be full, absolute or entire, having all the 'suchness' or modality that is worth having.

It must surely be obvious that the entirety of being which the argument postulates cannot be understood as an additive sum. The absolute Being cannot be simply an addition of all the positive beings and doings which ever could go on anywhere. He must be the existent Act of maximum richness and maximum elevation. I fought, and will fight to the last ditch, for the contention that active existence is thought of by us, and rightly thought of, as having levels of elevation and degrees of richness. But it is not clear that we are under any obligation to think of the 'scale of being' as running up to a determinate maximum. We can persuade ourselves to think so by concentrating on certain analogies, such as a series of decreasing defect approaching a norm. But it is not obvious that analogies of that sort are the right analogies to take. There seems to be no way of commanding general assent for the formula: 'The levels and modalities of all being which is thus or thus are graded by us as measures of Being just being itself.'

I saw the difficulty. I had to admit that the doctrine, thus abstractly stated, would never convince. But (I argued) nothing in so high and metaphysical a field of speculation ever will convince us, unless it is carried by an actual tendency, or dynamism, of our thought. Since, then, we do feel the force of the question 'Why is it so?' we cannot but acknowledge the vitality of the concealed motive which prompts the question; and that motive lies in the idea of sheer Being. It is nothing to be wondered at if the idea of the Supreme Existence in himself, outside and above the series of finites rising towards him, appears merely problematic to our minds; for the thought which erects the scheme places the supreme term outside the range of our experience. But in the question 'Why is it so?' pressed upon us by the contemplation of a finite existence, the finitising Infinite Cause makes his determinative act felt in the finite effect.

Such was the line of my defence. If it is to have any force, it requires an assumption to be made: the formalist account must be the only tolerable account that can be given of the motive concealed in the question. For then, if we take the question seriously, we are bound to take the formalist doctrine seriously. Whereas if an alternative account of the concealed motive is open to us, it is also open to us to take the question seriously while rejecting the formalist doctrine.

The doctrine has in fact betrayed itself by that very position of apparent strength in which it took refuge. 'In the question, *Why is it so?* as pressed upon us by the contemplation of a finite existence, the finitising Infinite Cause makes his determinative act felt in the finite effect.' Very well; but what is felt in the finite effect? A determining act; an act which (to escape an unending regress) must be purely originative, or sovereignly free. So in the last resort brute fact appears to our awestruck minds as the appointment of sheer, unconditioned choice. Now that a sheer and unconditioned choice is necessarily the act of 'Being just being itself in plenitude' is a proposition which might conceivably be true; but if so, it is a proposition which would need a distinct theorem to prove it. It is not a corollary directly to be granted by one who concludes to the act of a sovereign freedom.

When we have reached this point, we can no longer defer a reexamination of the 'Why is it so?' from which we started. Is it inevitable that we should accept the formalist account of what it means? If we see something arbitrary, something betraying external appointment, about any active existence's taking on any one form or modality, why should not we be contrasting it with the case of an existence which should clothe itself (its action, that is) with no form but the form it freely chooses?

And thus, proceeding from the 'Why is it so?' question, we may reach the God who is all he wills to be, and wills to be all he is: for his act is himself, and his act is free. And that is what we referred to as the voluntarist solution.

So, then, to conclude: there is no discord between our pragmatic theology and the argument *a contingentia mundi*, if it is allowed its proper logic. Both come to rest in the Unconditioned Will.

CHAPTER VIII

JUSTIFIABLE ANALOGY

THE conclusion we reached in the last chapter might seem to call for pious self-congratulation. How delightful, that metaphysical requirements and religious needs should square so nicely! And what a relief to be rid of that time-honoured headache, the logically necessary, or self-defining, super-essence! How much more concrete and meaningful, how much freer from logical scandal, is the thought of a wholly self-determining volition!

Perhaps; but we shall not get away with it so easily. The sceptical critic claims to be heard. 'I have no doubt' he says 'that the discomfort of sitting on one horn of a dilemma may awaken lively hopes of the cushioned ease its alternative horn affords; but the hopes are delusive. Sit there, and the horn will presently enter into your soul.

'The dilemma is this. The world's (supposed) dependence on God can be described either in abstract terms or in terms which are, by comparison, concrete. The advantage of abstract description is that it evades or at least minimises reliance on anthropomorphic analogy; its disadvantage is that it can be accused of vacuity. The advantage of the more concrete description is to evade the accusation of vacuity; its disadvantage, that it can never define or qualify the manlikeness in the divine nature on which it presumes to build.

'Allow me to enlarge a little on so formal an account of the dilemma I propose. When I speak of an abstract description of the world's dependence on God I do not mean a description which is highly general and in so far imperfect; I mean a description in which a highly abstract account is supposed to express what we essentially understand by the world's dependence upon God.

If to be logically contingent (i.e. to be a compost of brute fact) is to be dependent on that which is logically necessary (i.e. on a being luminously self-defined), then such highly abstract terms as I have just used serve best to express the very nature of the relation. That our account abstracts from the total natures of the entities involved, is obvious. We cannot meet a mammal coming up the road which is not also a horse, a dog or the like; and still less can we encounter a contingent being which is neither "animal, vegetable, nor mineral" but simply contingent. It is equally evident that "the necessary being" must have some character or content beside the mere property of being logically necessary. But the relation between the contingent and the necessary is supposed to be established by the mere contingency of the one, and the mere necessity of the other; and that being so, we are free to profess a certain detachment over the question, what further characteristics the necessary being has. No doubt we shall have our pious guesses; but our conviction of this Being's existence will be prior to them and independent of them. *If there is anything contingent, there is the Necessary.* So much is solid ground. Any attempt to characterise the subject of our conviction will have to fight with the admitted paradoxes of eminence, analogy and negation; but at least we shall have got something to characterise.

'The difficulty of this position is the vacuity, indeed, the logical monstrosity, of the very notion *necessary being*—the very suggestion that it is a description for which any reality could conceivably qualify. There is no need for me to labour a point which you appear to feel so strongly. Since you do so, you not unnaturally hasten to embrace the opposite alternative, and decide for a more concrete account of the whole relationship. To be contingent, you now suggest, is to be passively determined by agency other than one's own; and all contingents must ultimately be determined by the wholly free or self-determining agent, the sovereign will.

'You rejoice to claim that a will which makes its own choices and imposes them on others is not a vacuous notion, still less is it a logical monstrosity; and so you think you have shaken off the worst of your difficulties. You have indeed shaken off those difficulties; but only at the cost of incurring others no less troublesome. For you are now talking about the act of a rational will, about a real, full-blooded event, such as takes place when I act by choice, whether it be in thinking to myself, in talking to you, in working my limbs or in displacing environmental bodies. You are saying that such a voluntary activity, itself (I presume) disembodied, so acts as to bring into existence finite agents, tied to whatever modalities of action it may assign them. And the problem that confronts you is this: does it, or can it make any sense to put a voluntary act clean behind the world, and therefore divorced from every circumstance in which the operation of a voluntary act is intelligible to us?

'You will see now what I mean by my dilemma. I fear I have made it sound complicated; the principle involved is childishly simple. We cannot talk about God save in natural concepts, these being the only concepts which convey to us the notion of anything real. But our natural concepts cannot apply as they stand to a 'transcendent' God. Either, then, we attempt to extract a formula from them which will apply to deity neat; or else we hang on to the substance of the concepts we employ. In the first case we fall into vacuity, and are found to be offering no description of anything; in the second case we fall into anthropomorphism, and cannot fit our description to its transcendent subject.'

So far our critic. If it has been his purpose to show that both the positions he compares are beset with difficulty, we agree with him. If it has been his purpose to show that there is nothing to choose between the two, we cannot agree that this is what he has done. The two may both be difficult, without being equally bogus. Compare another dilemma. 'Either you assert freedom of decision or you deny it. Assert it, and you imply physical paradoxes; deny it, and you stultify moral reflection.' So what? We assert it, and we wrestle with the paradoxes. Dilemmas between problems and evasions are not balanced dilemmas; and such is the dilemma our critic sets before us.

The substance of theistic thought or reflection lies in the assertion of a higher analogue to rational will as primary determinator of all finite existence; and to wrestle with the problems which arise from such an assertion is to wrestle with the difficulties inherent in theism as such. And what is the evasive alternative? It is the pretence of settling the relatedness of finites to a divine ground without bringing into play the substantive theistic idea. It is very natural that so evasive a proceeding should prove vacuous. It is simply to be set aside as an unprofitable deviation, not dressed up as the dialectical opposite of the straight path from which it deviates.

We take it as axiomatic that the straight path of rational theology must be the prolongation of that basic theism which precedes all philosophising. It is a movement of thought which the simplest of minds can make; the rational theologian's justification must be that it calls for the development he gives it. As much, after all, can be said about our knowledge of our fellow-beings. The logic of the thought which allows a small child to appreciate his mother as a personal subject can be no miracle of complexity; it gives philosophers plenty to enlarge upon, nevertheless.

Theistic belief, needless to say, does not begin as pure speculation; but the strong practical interest it embodies is no reason for denying or neglecting the accompanying thought. Men cannot turn to supernatural beings for their advantage without conceiving both such beings and their own relation to them. What is philosophically important in this connexion is not the intriguing detail of primitive superstition but the flattest platitude of elementary reflection. The primitive believer has made the not very profound observation that while some part of his life and his situation is the direct creation of his voluntary choices, far too much neither is nor can be. He fumbles in his unenlightened way after the Decider or Deciders of those matters which he cannot himself either decide or control.

Out of this situation all sorts of possibilities can develop. On the side of religion, the true God (if you think so) may progressively show himself and be acknowledged; while at the same time the image of deity is threatened with every corruption by the projection upon it of men's foolish fancies or unregenerate desires. On the side of speculation, men will more and more observe that the proximate determinants of those factors in their lives which they cannot determine for themselves are other finite agents with whom they share the world. At the same time they will be coming to see that none of these other agents is any more self-determining than they themselves are, and most of them vastly less so; and the undetermined Determinator, the Sovereign Will and ultimate Power, is acknowledged to stand behind or above the whole series of finite determinants and determinates.

Such, in a few words, is the matrix of theistic reflection; it can be greatly refined upon, and debated up and down; but it is a very conceited thing to imagine one can disown it in essence without renouncing theism itself. And central to the whole development from start to finish is that voluntarist account of deity which is so irredeemably analogical. The primitive believer in gods might think them to be not all that different from himself; when, however, we have thought the matter out to the end, we cannot escape from some such formula as this: Deity is as-it-were personal will, of so exalted a form as to be simply undetermined *a priori* in any respect.

The logical scandal here is that 'Deity' stands for precisely that analogical notion which the appended description proceeds to set out. It is not like saying 'Dancing is the as-it-were poetry of motion', when we know already what the act of dancing is, before we attach the analogical description to it. Influenced by such a comparison, we very naturally look for some method of establishing 'Deity' independently of any analogical statement. It was this that the argument to Necessary Being attempted unsuccessfully to do.

If we consider the model we have just taken, we can distinguish three ways in which the sense of 'dancing' might be established independently of analogical description: (a) by proper definition

(b) by ostensive indication (c) by performance. I know what it is to dance; it is (a) to take a series of steps etc. (b) to do what he and she are doing over there (c) to go like this . . . Of these three methods, the argument to Necessary Being tried to arrive at (a), laying down a non-analogical definition of deity. It proved abortive. Perhaps something more like (b) or (c) would offer better hopes.

By way of preliminary we have to point out that the model imperfectly fits the case. 'Personal will, *but of so exalted a form as* . . .' does not function like 'Poetry, *but of motion.*' We do not mean to say that dancing is poetry at all; we mean to say that what poetry is to language, dancing is to personal movement. Whereas we do mean to say that deity is personal will; only that we cannot conceive such a voluntary person as should enjoy the freedom and originativeness of First Causality.

This distinction having been duly noted, we may venture to take up the three methods of giving proper value to a term standing for a personal action. Of the three, the last is surely basic. If we could do nothing towards dancing, we should not know in any full sense what it is for a person to dance. We might, indeed, be incapable of any dancing that deserved the name. Yet we should still know what it was to make movements or gestures; and so we should be able to conceive the taking of movements in rhythmic pattern or series, as (b) we see those performers to do whom we vainly aspire to imitate. And so we should be able to state and understand a definition (a), which mentioned movements such as we can make (c), adapted to the execution of figures such as we observe (b).

To take the extreme case—is there a man paralysed almost from birth, with no effective use of his limbs, able to do little more than wag his head and work his mouth? Then his sense of what it would be to dance will surely be most imperfect, his whole direct experience of voluntary movement being so rudimentary. But that limitation need not make the idea of dancing totally unreal to him. On the contrary, his own incapacity may endow with a vivid interest that combination of freedom and control which dancing exhibits. He may realise in watching a ballet an intensity of delight inseparable from painful contrast, such as no normal spectator could share.

We proceed to apply the three methods to the theological case. We take (c) first. I cannot perform the voluntary act of First Causation, but I can perform voluntary acts; acts, moreover, which have in them something originative. My action cannot reach the elevation or intensity of First Act, but I can push it upwards, as it were in that direction; I can rise from quite rudimentary performances to the most distinctively personal or rational activity I am capable of; and the idea of going further is one which I readily entertain. The distance which separates my best performances from the Sovereign Freedom goes against adequacy of understanding on my part, but not against reality of concern; a concern like that of the cripple, characterised by a strained aspiration.

Not, indeed, that we take the notion of deity to be an ideal of our own action, which we are prevented from overtaking by an accidental defect. It is the notion of a Being and Agent whose sphere we cannot share; and this fact may seem to throw all the more weight on (b), ostensive indication. Divine efficacy is not simply what mine would be, but for a certain paralysis. Is it perhaps what is displayed in 'God's handiwork', the existence of the created world? We cannot, of course, point to divine act; but neither can we point to finite personal act outside ourselves; we can point only to its phenomenal evidences. I cannot see another person exercise the voluntary performance of dancing, because the voluntary execution of conduct is performed, not seen. I cannot feel *him* dance, even if he dances on my toe. What I have is an immediate and inescapable supposition of his dancing (in the personal sense) when the evidence hits me. It so presses the supposition upon me as virtually to require it.

The paralysed man's feeling for personal movement is stretched and patterned by the sight of dancing figures; the believer's sense for creative volition is formed and stretched by the contemplation of God's handiwork. So far as it goes, the parallel is just; for we do understand by God a voluntary power originative enough and comprehensive enough for the absolute production of all things created, as they are either perceived, inferred or conjectured by us. Where the parallel fails is in the matter of the compulsion exercised by the supposition, once granted the evidence. We are virtually unable not to suppose personal action, as a reality finding expression in the phenomena of personal conduct; whereas, with all the furniture of heaven and earth before his vision, the unilluminated can still say, 'There is no God'.

If we wish to understand the predicament of belief, it will be of use to consider what it is that makes the supposition of other-personal activity so compulsive. It might seem natural for this purpose to examine the criteria by which we implicitly do, or scientifically should, distinguish phenomena disclosing other-personal activity from phenomena which make no such disclosure. But that line of enquiry would carry us beside the mark. Religious thought has no interest in distinguishing God-revealing facts from facts that do not show his hand at all. Its distinctions run on other lines—say between facts revealing different levels or strands of divine purpose, or between facts whose revelatory message is plain and those which are opaque to us. Besides, whether relevant or irrelevant to our theological parallel, the criteria for picking out person-disclosing phenomena are not the keys to our reason for believing in one another's personal existence. That reason lies in a broader consideration, to which therefore we will turn.

Mentality as we know it is a social product. Thought is the interiorisation of dialogue. We should not think at all, were we not mutually aware. Speech is the standard case of mutual communication; but speech is merely a specialised form of intentional action directed at one's fellows, and the understanding of speech presupposes acknowledgement of other-personal activity as such. It is not possible to be a mind which neither accepts nor has accepted other-personal activity for what it is. We live that belief, and only are what we are by so doing.

To make the theological parallel watertight we should need to say that God has conferred on us a form of existence of which the exercise is inseparable from a lived belief in God, pursued in personal relation to divine personality. But on the theistic hypothesis itself it is scarcely possible to make out such a claim, so far at least as our natural existence is concerned. For God is held to be the universal Cause of Nature, not a particular factor in natural existence. He constitutes the world a system of self-existent things, interacting with one another by their inborn principles. Reflection seeks a first Cause, aspiration feels after a supreme Good; but we can pursue reasonable aims without acknowledging divine vocation and understand the causal structure of events without attending to First Causality.

On the believing hypothesis, all men are in actual dependence on the divine will for their existence and their calling. But it is false to claim, as Berkeley on his own ground was bold to do, that our knowledge of God through our evident dependence on his action is as indubitable as our knowledge of one another. Were our knowledge of one another simply inferential, we might make out some sort of case. The theological inference has not the same grounds of close and intelligible analogy to go upon as the inference to other human selves, God's action in all nature not being so recognisably human and personal as other men's in their conduct. But one might try to plead with Berkeley that the uniquely originative force of first causality, implied in all occurrence, indicates 'Spirit' as powerfully as analogy of conduct indicates it in the phenomena of our neighbours' action. Even supposing the plea could be made out (and it scarcely can be, without the support of Berkeley's darling fallacies) it is still beside the point. For our general ground for believing in other selves is not simply inferential; it is that we are the selves we are by living the belief.

Without the belief we could not be the persons we are. We could have been mindless imbeciles, though, and still remained innocent of all communication; and that would have been existence of a sort. It is the personal enhancement of what would otherwise by a merely physiological functioning, that is dependent on the lived belief in communicators. The proper theological analogy would be, presumably, a further enhancement beyond the personally human; a level of action equally inseparable from dealings with a Person believed in, the Person in this case being divine. Such an enhancement of being has of course been claimed, and has received from its participants splendid names; it is eternal life, or just 'life' as the sole condition worth contrasting with death; it is life-in-God.

That life-in-God is the function of relation to God is a tautology; and that the relation supposes belief in God, is a plain corollary. The evidential difficulty is that of making life-in-God an undeniable reality, like sheer personal existence. The difficulty is both logical and moral. To take the logic first; a man who denies the personality which is membership in a society of discourse contradicts himself; for a denial is a linguistic and a personal act. A man who denies life-in-God does not contradict himself; for if there could be minds out of all relation to the divine, they could still make denials. The moral difficulty is that believers must confess the poverty of their responses to an Infinite Object. 'Eternal life' is so-called because our enjoyment of it in this temporal scene is the merest foretaste. The evidence of it lies less in our effective exercise of it than in the divine quality of what we touch, when our apprehensions are liveliest.

This last consideration finds expression in a whole range of analogy drawn from a different realm, the aesthetic. We talk of glimpses or visions of the divine, analogous to occasional intense perceptions of aesthetic beauty or appreciations of poetic significance. Such comparisons have their uses, but they bear rather on the fitfulness or the movingness of the experience than on its subject-matter. That which is so suddenly moving, and surrounds itself with such an aureole, is an effect referred to God as to its creative source or its underlying subject. And while the contemplative reference to God of events or objects outside our control is often deeply moving to pious minds, the substance of the matter lies in the reference to God of our own action. It is that direct relating of will to will, or of thought to thought, which we have discussed in earlier chapters.

What we have been saying comes down to the platitude that God is the object of faith. Faith can be philosophised upon, for it can be shown that the nature of the believer's evidences is such as his hypothesis either allows or demands; and the demonstration of that requires a purely logical treatment. What cannot be shown is that the life of faith—which is life-in-God—has that unquestionable validity which attaches to life in community. At the same time the difference must not be exaggerated. It is not as though we believed in our neighbours' personality *because* logical philosophers are able to exhibit the self-contradiction involved in denying it. From first infancy our elders loved us, played us, served us, talked us into knowing them; and so the believer claims that he has been brought by mediated divine initiatives into the knowledge of God. That his 'knowledge' does not allow of the logical proofs available in the other sphere, lies in the nature of the case.

It is time we retraced our steps. Let us go back to the point at which we observed that the temptingness of 'necessary being' theology lay in its appeal to a perfectly logical desire: the desire to establish divine existence independently of any analogising from finite to infinite person or spirit. We set aside the 'necessary being' approach, but hoped to find along some other line what that argument failed to give. The comparison and the contrast provided by the example of understanding personal movement have shown us that there is no question of our bypassing analogy; for to think about God is to think of living act, to which our own action is the only possible clue; and it is a clue which falls so short that it must be stretched by a bafflingly great analogical extension. There is, then, no thought of God without analogy; but there is in the believer's eyes a dealing with God which is no mere interpretation of nature through a strained analogical scheme, but an enjoyment of 'life-in-God', which is to him self-authenticating. It is a reality not to be objectively observed (how could it be?) but performed or lived; and so the believer escapes from dependence on mere analogical inference in the same way as the believer in other-personal existence escapes from it; for he lives the belief, a belief which, admittedly, has an analogical shape. At the same time it must be admitted that life-in-God has not the indubitable evidence of life-in-community.

We may seem to have shifted our ground in the course of our discussion. We set out to stop a leak in an argument from universal contingency; we end by putting our trust in a dimension or enhancement of the believer's own existence. Even supposing the second reason for conviction will hold water, what does it do towards patching the first? Are we saying any more than has been said so often—that the arguments of rational theology being proved valueless, we should build our faith on 'religious experience'?

I hope we have not said anything quite so banal. Our position is that theism must be lived as well as thought; and equally that without being thought it cannot be lived. The very form of 'life-in-God' is voluntary acceptance of a Creative Will which has a scope in principle universal. It is an experiment (if the word can be endured) in drawing upon First Causality; and if anything has a First Cause, everything has. It is platitudinous to point out that we cannot experiment in any creature's causedness save our own. But what we experimentally realise is a relation having the structure which the contingency argument exploits. Our self knowledge offers in this regard both a just illumination and a solid support to our understanding of the status of our fellow-creatures. Their contingency, or non-self-explanitoriness, can be discussed on its own ground rationally enough. The brute-fact character of things can be swallowed; it can scarcely be disputed. To swallow it is much the same thing as to denounce for fantastic or vacuous that ultimate explanation, or First Causality, to which the life of belief gives substance and application.

CHAPTER IX

FIRST CAUSE

THEISM, as we have seen, begins from a simple acknowledgement of Supernatural person or will, as sovereign over those
matters which human decision cannot arrange. Further reflection
calls attention to the many finite causes which are the proximate
determinants of our existence. If men continue to believe in
God, it will be because they do not allow to finite causes, whether
remote or near, the sheer originativeness of 'First Causality'. It is
inevitable that, sooner or later, such a refusal should take the
form of an argument. Finite causes are put forward as sufficient
of themselves to account for the 'phenomena'. Their pretensions
are denied and causality is pushed back into the Infinite. So God
comes to be seen as the First Cause transcending all natural
causes.

If we survey the whole historical phenomenon of theistic
belief we may be inclined to view preoccupation with finite
causes as a mere episode which can be bracketed out of the
story. We end where we begin—with personal will sovereign
over affairs; finite causes claimed to do the job but their pretensions have been exploded. Such may be the Olympian view
of an orthodox historian of doctrine, casting an eye over the
millennia; it is unlikely to be the view of minds involved in the
battle of ideas and working their way back out of naturalism
into theism. They do not begin with a Zeus, whose functions
have been absurdly usurped by Stellar Gyration. They begin with
natural causes, which are for them the typical forms of explanation; and when argument drives the explanatory search beyond
the natural world, the First Cause they posit wears a physio-
morphic guise; there will be need of further argument to justify

the painting of personal traits into the picture; and even then people will be found complaining that the Supreme Being of philosophy is not the God of Religion.

Since it is not possible to bar *a priori* the claim of natural explanations to explain, philosophical theologians seem bound to accept the naturalistic starting point, however far they may hope to progress beyond it; and so the philosophy of causes becomes a theological concern. Here a further field of debate opens; for philosophical theologians differ markedly as to the degree in which they assimilate the sorts of explanation offered by natural and by First Causality respectively. A full account of disagreements on this head would require a formidable treatise. We will content ourselves with a broad classification.

The simplest and most tempting approach is perhaps the Cartesian. The state of physical theory in the latter part of the Seventeenth Century made it easy to emphasise the utter disparity between body and Spirit. Body could do nothing but pass on imparted motion according to billiard-ball rules; and so it was obvious that a scientist pursuing physical explanations in physical terms could never explain how anything happened at all; only Spirit could be a true motor. The scientific basis for the Cartesian approach has now disappeared; and in any case the theologian has small reason to shed tears over the loss of it. If it made the proof of a creator fallaciously evident, it removed every intelligible reason why he should have ever created. What could eternal wisdom gain, by willing into existence wooden dummies of his own geometrical ideas, and stirring them round in space?

If we are to have a world worth creating—a universe of creatures in the old sense—it must be allowed that their Creator has imparted to them some measure of his own active and causative power. If this is conceded, it is still possible to take divergent paths. It can be held that the mode and nature of action on the part of physical creatures, though real, are still so diverse from the Creative Act, that there is no natural transition from physical to theological explanation; and so the universe and our reasonable thoughts about it stand as an alien block between spiritual man and divine Spirit. Or it can be held that all created energies are in so far little models of the one Omnipotence, that the questions asked of them and incompletely answered by them can be carried back much as they are to receive a fuller satisfaction from the Prime Causality. The first alternative is the view of godly men who find an obstacle in what they take to be a godless science. The second alternative though requiring careful qualification, we hold to be nearer the truth; it is in fact implied in the account our last chapter gave of the 'Why is it so?' question. Things have a limited power to make themselves and their fellow-beings what they are; because this power acts always within preordained limits, we look for the unlimited Power or Will which has initially ordained all things.

We talk of several doctrines of causality—not that, strictly speaking, there ought to be a theory of causes, as though causes were a class of events, or even as though cause-and-effect described a class of natural relations. Causes are named by reference to our quest for grounds of explanation; but the relation of the event or action we explain to the event or action from which we explain it, and which is called its cause, is not a relation of one determinate type called 'causal dependence'. To take but one distinction: the cause of a certain phase of activity may be found in the previous phase of which it is the continuation or development; but then again the cause may be found in the interference of an alien activity producing a change in the activity we are considering. And it is surely plain that continuity with one's own previous phase, and reaction to interferences, are not examples of an identical relation.

We are sometimes recommended to call 'the cause of an event' that complex of preceding factors which suffices to assure us it will take place. Very well; and if anyone likes to use 'cause' in that sense, good luck to him. But such a usage of the word, if adopted, is no good reason for confusing the very different types of relation which tie into the 'causal' complex the elements composing it. Let the complex be the cause; but if it causes, it does so in virtue of the various continuities and interferences of force or action which make it up; not through any magic attaching to the complex pattern as such.

The recommended usage we have just mentioned may be convenient; it would be a pity to give it exclusive right. For 'cause' has its special value as an ambiguous term, referring to events or actions in so far as they serve for explanation; we do not analyse the structure of process in terms of cause-and-effect.

What we have to examine is the structure of action and inter-action; and what should we know about either, apart from our exercise of action on our own account? My own act, of which I am myself the voluntary author, is my standing example of activity; and I become aware of environmental activities or forces in so far as they engage with mine. I am bound to think of the activities with which I engage as being in some sense *in pari materia* with my own; even though I am obliged to make a discount of uncertain amount in transferring my conception of my own action to the credit of natural forces or agents. They are not conscious, they are not voluntary, and yet they act; their act is their existence and they have a place somewhere in that scale of agency which spans creation and, in its upward reach, points on through man towards God.

I have written at large on this theme elsewhere and do not wish to repeat what was perhaps sufficiently expressed. What I pro-pose to do now is to make a slight review of Aristotle's causal doctrine from the standpoint of the distinctions we have drawn. Where does his theory stand, in relation to these distinctions? And what has been its effect on the notion of First Causality held by orthodox theology?

A glance suffices to show that the Aristotelian pattern of the four causal factors was extracted from the model of human action—to be precise, the model of a craftsman doing carpentry. If anything is to be made, there must be some *deal* (for that, literally, is what the Latin word 'matter' and its Greek prototype signify). The job consists in bringing the deal into the required *shape* (form); and this will not happen without a *making agent* to do it, nor will he set to work without a *purpose* to aim at. Having picked his four factors, the Philosopher applies them with his famous analogical subtlety to the analysis of every process in heaven or on earth. But however far the analogy is stretched, man is the model; and as we are ourselves maintaining human action as the sole inevitable clue to any conception of natural efficacy we can form, it is of interest to observe the originator of natural philosophy in Europe striking into the same path.

As with most Aristotelian doctrines, the development was Aristotle's, the seminal idea was Plato's. That any causality must be a sort of carpentry is the assumption underlying a truly astounding text in his *Timaeus*. Having drawn the familiar distinction between the changeless eternal, and the changing which comes to be and perishes, Timaeus continues: 'Everything that comes to be must come to be under the action of a cause. The product, then, whereof the artificer has his eye on the changeless, using a model of that kind and expressing its form and force in his work, is bound to turn out well. Not so the product of one with his eye on the coming-to-be, and employing a model of that nature.' Having thus calmly begged the question whether all causation is or is not a sort of carpentry, Timaeus proceeds without more ado to discourse upon the cosmic carpenter, the artificer of the world. The status of so mysterious a being has been much debated by commentators on the Master's work. Is he to be taken as a real person or as an expository convenience? Perhaps the question did not arise for Plato quite in that form. The world has a cause; and causation is a sort of carpentry. One can get on with an exposition of the world's genesis in carpentry terms, without pinpointing the causal agent; as indeed Timaeus virtually declares a few lines below.

The masters of ancient philosophy, then, took it that causation was to be understood by the clue of the agency we ourselves exercise; and they were right, for we have no other clue to it. They grievously erred, nevertheless, and misled the mind of Europe. Their error lay in jumping the gap between the carpenter's project and its realisation. To describe what the car-

penter does as the imposition of form upon deal is mythical.
The carpenter bears the form in mind, but what he does to the
deal is to hack it, whether with chisel, saw, or plane. The several
acts of hacking are the acts he immediately intends and directly
executes; and it is here that his encounter with external nature
takes place. Deal makes no reaction to the imposition of table-
form as such; it reacts to the strokes of the chisel, sometimes
splitting, sometimes cutting true, sometimes resisting, according
as the grain runs or the tool is aimed. The organisation of detail
by form belongs to the carpenter's conduct, not to any physical
event. It is true that when he has finished, his materials form
up into the shape he intends; but their doing so is nothing to
them.

Here is a parable. A foreign expert distinguished in his own
eyes but not in those of my fellow citizens announces his intention
to visit our museum on a certain day. Struck by the indecorum
of his presence passing without public notice, I give twenty
different people twenty different motives for coming there at
the time; and this I do by promising each of them the sight of
a different object of special interest to him, not currently kept on
public display. The twenty come. My intention of having a
crowd to meet the great man is fulfilled; but it casts no light
whatever on the reactive properties of the human material composing the crowd. They have displayed reactive properties, sure
enough, but to cultural interest, not to diplomatic duty; to
personal hobbyism, not to the formation of an assembly. To
describe the twenty before they assemble as 'potentially a re-
ception committee' is in a sense true, since we can scarcely deny
the scholastic maxim which validates the inference back from
'is' to 'could be'. But it is about as vacuous a truth as truth can be.
No more vacuous, however, than the description of the carpenter's deal as 'potentially a table'.

No wonder Aristotle's natural philosophy provided no recipe
for fruitful experiment. We learn little enough about natural
substances by seeing whether they are receptive of the forms we
design for them. The Aristotelian will think with complacency

of materials so selected or so prepared that their reactions can be taken for granted; like the modeller's clay, they are mere matter to our purposes. Even here there is more to it than the onlooker imagines, and the Greek modeller knew better than the Greek philosopher. Clay had its quality, and modelling was a battle with it; his business, he said, was with the moment when the clay was up his nails; not, that is, with the detachment of comtemplative design.

If we discount material reactions and see ourselves as imposing a form, what we take to be our action passes over the heads of the natural agents and nowhere engages them on a level. But in fact to impose a form we must descend into the arena and engage brute agents hand to hand, undergoing their pressures and inflicting ours. And that is a business we are engaged in anyhow, and not only when we attempt manufacture. We must overcome the contrary pull of any weight we try to lift, we must push against the wind when we walk, we must chew our food when we eat it. It is by action that we taste the counter-action of natural forces, and in terms of action that we must interpret them.

So long as we hold fast to the carpenter's hacking and fitting, his work remains essentially personal. But once we abstract from these homely actions, we can abstract from the carpenter himself. Form (existent in the carpenter's mind) reproduces itself in the finished article; the carpenter is needed only as a place for the form to perch, before it moves on into the deal. Presumably Aristotle would never have thought in this way, if he had been simply concerned to describe carpenters. In fact his concern was with nature, and he wanted a formula abstract enough to be applicable outside the human sphere. He designs to show what sort of carpentry nature does; and of course nature's 'carpentry' is not carpentry.

So the aspect of the model which he retains is this: that in process the material *becomes* what the carpenter's thought *is*. Mental being is, certainly, being of a mysterious and paradoxical kind; thought, says the Philosopher, somehow *is* all that is thinkable. Physical being is more straightforward; any given thing has a limited and definable form which makes it what it is. It is causally active in virtue of that form; form infects or colours its environment, through processes in which things possessed of the requisite receptivity take on its colour or become in some measure what it is.

So causality goes from being to becoming. We start with being. Granted that a thing characterised by a given definable essence exists, why it possesses an attribute belonging to its essence is not a question. Its having such an attribute belongs to its being what it is. But the essences of things in this world not only prescribe essential attributes, they allow of accidental qualities. Iron must be heavy; it may be hot. It may be, but why in any given case is it so? Through the influence of another substance already possessing heat. And to stop an infinite regress in explanation, we must postulate somewhere a substance essentially possessed of any characteristic accruing to other things accidentally. Flame (for example) is essentially hot; other things are accidentally so through its direct or indirect influence. They are hot, once they have become hot, and so long as the causal influence which makes them so persists. They take time to heat up, and so there is process or alteration in things; a time during which 'agents' are causing change, and 'patients' are undergoing it.

Such is the basic scheme. Taken as it stands, it leaves many things unexplained; for example, the birth and decay of substances themselves. For the essential forms which make substances to be the substances they are seem to be as accidental to the brute matter of the universe as accidental qualities are to substances already existing. Explanation must be sought further back and higher up. The steps of ascent backwards up the causal stair are not quite the same for Aristotle's Christian disciples as they are for the Philosopher; but however they are counted they will bring us to a First Cause which is a superessence standing above all accidentality. It radiates causal influence, it undergoes none. It exhaustively characterises a Being which simply and completely is what it is, immutably self-defined in all respects, and owing to its form alone whatever can be truly predicated of it.

The sketch we have drawn may serve to bring out the straight-forward relation between a formalist theory of natural causes and a theology of absolute essence. But we have made a cruel simplification of ideas which were nothing if not flexible and comprehensive. The worst or anyhow the most relevant of the injustices we have done to Aristotle lies in what we said, or failed to say, about the rôle of activity in his system. The subject is by no means exhausted by a mention of the causal influence of 'agent' substances upon 'patient' substances. It is an active business for substances fully to be what they are or to realise their natures. Changeable beings like us will actualise themselves through successive exploitations of environmental opportunity. Not so, of course, the first and changeless Being. His life is indeed supremely active, but his activity is not a process of self-realisation; it is the perfect and timeless possession of the content his essence implies. Freedom of choice finds its place in Aristotle's system, but not at the level of divine existence. It is the dis-cretionary adaptation of means to ends on the part of a changeable being in pursuit of its own fulfilment. The supreme Being doubt-less has supreme freedom, since he immediately and timelessly does all that a rational mind can wish to achieve. But his freedom is not expressed in decision, nor is it creative. Aristotelism accommodates activity within a framework of essence. Essence gives activity its aim, and the Supreme Activity is supremely expressive of the essence which it perpetually actualises.

The adaptation of Aristotle to Christian uses inevitably raised a certain tension between the causality of essence and the efficacy of decision; since for Christians the good-pleasure of God was the determinant of all creation. Various Scholastics went far in a voluntaristic or arbitrarian direction; but the old essentialism was never extirpated. Metaphysics remained rooted in physics, and the Aristotelian account of physical causes was the most serviceable to be had until Galileo and Newton displaced it.

Even when it was expelled from physics, the old formalism continued to hang about theology. Two reasons can be given for such an anomaly. On the one side, *vis inertiae*. Men did not feel the same practical urgency about reconstruction at the top of their system as they felt about it at the bottom; physics demanded innovation; theology could comfortably run in well-worn grooves. On the other side, the inapplicability of the causal concepts apparently demanded by the new science. Where the Aristotelian concepts had a built-in elasticity, stretching to cover every sort of case, the new physical concept was rigid, and limited to a one-level field. So the ghost of an Aristotelian theology continued to haunt a Newtonian universe. Kant was still struggling with it in the Critique of Pure Reason and (to descend from the sublime to the ridiculous) so was the author of *Finite and Infinite*.

There can be no pleasure in blackguarding the supreme educator of the European mind and first creator of exact philosophy. The introduction of Aristotle's categories into theology itself gave it the chance to become a rational discipline. Nevertheless I think it right to say that Aristotelian causal theory has been the bane of rational theology for more than half a millennium. I would say, Aristotelian causal theory, not any perverse delight in absolutism for its own sake, nor any rage for mere metaphysical hyperbole about the divine Being. Feeling that there is something ungodly about the traditional position, modern philosophers, such as Professor Charles Hartshorne, have made a direct demand for a more imaginably personal account of the godhead. Hartshorne certainly makes effective points; but a crusade so conceived can scarcely lead to a decisive victory. Good reasons for steering wide of Charybdis may bring the navigator under the jaws of Scylla; every theologian is bound to find a course between anthropomorphism and ineffability; and perhaps if God is to be God he cannot be as intelligible to man as Hartshorne would have him. We are on firmer ground if we work out First Causality from first principles. Granting the Aristotelian interpretation of cause and, in consequence, of prime cause, it is not easy to see

the 'metaphysical absolutism' as anything but a proper inference. If we follow a different causal path, we shall reach a
different conception of the First Cause; no less 'hyperbolical',
perhaps, but perhaps less static or depersonalised.

CHAPTER X

ANIMA MUNDI

WE have made a comparison between causal systems, and especially two, one formalist, the other activist; the Aristotelian, and that which on our part we wish to commend. Aristotle placed being before becoming, and so came back to a first being who simply and absolutely was. We place determinators before determinates, and so come back to a determinator who is nothing but what he determines to be—a free Spirit. But whatever considerations we have been able to advance in favour of our system we have so far cast little if any light on the nature of the causal relation—the joint, as it were—between the action of the First Determinator, and the finite activities determined by him.

When we were discussing the interpretation of existence which is of practical concern to religion, we were happy to point out that the joint just referred to does not come into question. For man's business is to set himself in the line of the divine intention, not to manage a contact with supernatural force or transcendent process. We believe that, being conformed to the will of God, we are used by him in the way such conformity expresses. The divine operation is God's secret; the effect is displayed in what we are enabled to do. It may be a tolerable language to describe our action as a cooperation with God; but such cooperation is nothing like cooperation with our fellow-beings, when our work and their work dovetail together in specifiable ways. On occasion, we may accept the action of other finite agents as the work of God, and set ourselves to dovetail with it; but it is evident that instances of the sort cast no light on our problem. The mystery is, how the action of any finite agents, whether severally or jointly, is subject to the causality of God.

An austere empiricism might decide that what does not enter into the pattern of our active concern is nothing to us; and that having no experimental evidence on which to settle the question, we cannot meaningfully raise it. But an empiricism so abrupt as this is surely self-stultifying. For the activity we can exercise in relation to God is so far comparable with the relations we culti-vate towards our neighbour, that it supposes belief in him as in a person whose will so acts that we can embrace it. And a belief without which practice is impossible, cannot be called wholly unpractical. We live the belief, and in so doing, we cannot leave it utterly undefined. The idea of the relation of our activity to God's causality cannot play its part in our imaginations while remaining to us just 'some relatedness, we know not what'. It is at least so far definitely conceived by us as to exclude certain accounts of it; for example, it cannot be the simple relation of part to whole; for if our will or action is a mere part of God's, we can have no adjustment to make of ours to his.

However else the relation may be viewed, it is taken to be a moral relation; that is, it is assimilated to relation with our neighbour, whatever qualifications may be appended. One might say, Relation to another active self, only not 'out there' but (as has recently been claimed) 'in the ground of our being'. Or should we say 'In the springing-point of our act'? The phrase may strike us as less opaque, but it is no less composed of gross physical metaphor. It represents our activity as a jet of water spreading from the fine aperture through which a pressure below, invisible to us, forces it; or as a shoot thrown out from the parent stem by a life invisible beneath the cover of the bark. Such metaphors serve only to place the Creator's act in sheer priority to ours; a priority which is of no less concern to a theology of nature than it is to a theology of grace.

Should not a philosopher try to do better? Perhaps analogical terms cannot be avoided; it should nevertheless be possible to discard gross metaphor. We may not have a primary concern for the perfect clarification of notions admittedly metaphysical, which do not give immediate shape to our action. Yet the secondary concern we have is not negligible, if our religious existence is in some sense a living of our belief in a causality passing over from Infinite into finite act.

'Ought not you to go further?' says our critic. 'Can you, as a theologian, admit that your concern here is secondary in any degree? You are not, I take it, prepared to have the religious life simply reduced to the moral; you see it as a life of obedience to an actual God. But it appears to me that you hope to draw a line between your conception of God (for that, if anything is, must be of primary importance to a theologian) and your conception of his efficacy in determining his creatures. And I cannot see how such a line can be drawn. You cannot pretend to know God except as Creator—creator of finite entities, or of further perfections or achievements in such entities. And Creation is a sort of efficacy; your Creator is one who exercises it, as the baker is one who bakes. The verb defines the noun, the action reveals the agent. A baker does not become a baker by being the *cause* of bread, (say) on the supposition that he grows it on trees in the form of breadfruit. That would not be baking, it would be fruitfarming.

'You tell me that you work very happily in your religion with the idea of a Person whose will is determinative and to be embraced. I want to know whether this is poetry, commenting, I dare say fruitfully, on the moral destiny of man; or serious doctrine, enshrining in analogical language a core of metaphysical belief. You reply that if theology is a mythology, it is mythology about a God taken to be non-mythical; it is not a God-mythology about mundane realities. If asked to justify your statement, you reply that the divine action is taken as the cause of mundane activities, never as the exercise of them. Very well; let *cause* be the lifeblood of your faith. But what do you mean by cause in this connexion? Cause, we have agreed, is a mere generic term for an act, circumstance or event which in any way serves to explain what occurs. How, then, can you be convinced of the operation of a cause, unless you can specify the way it operates?

'Consider the following dialogue: Why did you get in the way of the traffic?—A girl caused me to step off the pavement.—How did she do that? Did she push you? Did she so walk that you stepped aside to give her room? Did she ask you to do it? Did her charms, glimpsed on the other side of the street, draw you across the roadway? Or strike you all of a heap, so that you lost control of your feet?—No, it was none of these things—What was it, then?—I can't say; but I am sure it was a girl made me do it.

'What are we to make of such an answer? It could only hope to pass as the record of an imperfect memory. He made a mental note at the time that it was a girl who caused it; how, he can no longer recall. But evidently our claim that God is the universal First Cause cannot represent imperfect memory of this sort, unless it be on the strength of Plato's myth—that the soul was clearer-sighted in a previous existence, and able to observe what she now confusedly remembers.

'Indeed my parable was too favourable to the agnostic believer in divine causality. For the girl on the pavement is a girl, however it may have been about her diverting you into the roadway. But a creator is not a creator irrespective of his creating. To make the parallel strict, we should need to rewrite the conversation on a level of utter futility: What diverted your steps into the roadway?—I was diverted by a divertent.—Meaning by a divertent, what?—An agency which diverted.—Diverted in what way?—Not in any way rather than in any other.'

Ah, but now you have let yourself be carried away by the pleasures of satire. You have forgotten the conditions of the question before us. Had we not agreed that the practice of religion and the logic of theistic reflection are at one in seeing the Primary Determinant as personal will? This being so, the specification of the causal relation is not as crucial an issue as you allege. Your parable will need to be reconstructed. You take it to be a person who made you step off the pavement, and you take that person to have meant you to do what he made you do. There is only one point which remains undecided—how his meaning you to act came to bear in causing you to act. And, in the human case, that is an issue we often leave unexplored. If, for example, we were told that one of Queen Elizabeth the First's courtiers broke off an intended marriage because such was the royal will, we might not trouble to enquire how the sovereign displeasure was brought home to him.

'I dare say; but then there are several easily imaginable ways in which the Queen could make her wishes felt; if you are uncertain, it is because you do not know which of several perfectly adequate suppositions to adopt. In the theological case, it is all we can do to think of one which tolerably fits. Still, I do not see that we need despair. I was arguing against pious agnosticism, by reducing it *ad absurdum*. I am still entitled to argue in favour of positive belief. Let us take the question up on the terms you have just laid down. The hypothesis shall be that a personal activity of mind or will, all-embracing in scope, determines the many particular acts of the world's constituents; and the question shall be, What model do we possess for such a scheme? Surely there is no need for us to look far afield. Does not every act of rational volition do what we suppose the divine will to do? We know nothing of any will or mind existing or acting otherwise than by the employment of a bodily instrument. And to use a bodily instrument means bringing into play a great number of bodily constituents, which so act by their own proper motion as to further the voluntary purpose. Will you not wish to say, then, that as my mind is the mind of my body, so God's will is the soul of the world?'

Thank you for so positive a suggestion. We shall need to look at it with some care. But there is one point in the relation you propose for comparison which offers immediate consolation; and that is its unintelligibility. We believe the body to be a physiological system organising a vast number of minute parts. We have no insight whatever into the way in which our act of will directs their multiple activities. Yet we have a practical belief that it

146

does so. Thus it is plain that an ignorance of the mode by which will fulfils itself in its instruments is no bar to a conviction that it does so fulfil itself. Where I am the universal operator in my microcosm, I have no awareness of the relation by which I determine the cellular operators; where I am a cellular operator in the macrocosm, I have no awareness of the relation by which the universal operator determines me.

But I do not think you invoked the analogy to justify a pragmatic agnosticism; you meant on the contrary, to define the nature of the creature-creator relation as nearly as possible. If your positive contention holds good, it will carry an important consequence for metaphysics; it will mean that the proper form for theism to take is a Philosophy of Total Organism. If that is the thesis we have to consider, we ought to scrutinise somewhat closely the parallel on which it is built. Is it as persuasive on a second view as it seems at first sight? There are certainly radical differences between the matters you have so confidently compared.

On either side there is thought and will (mine, God's) and a plurality of constituents (the cells etc. of my body, the things constitutive of the universe). On either side the thought is taken to rule the constituent parts. So far, perhaps, so good. But we have just observed that thoughtful purpose in ourselves rules the multitude of its bodily constituents by ignoring them. The actions I heedfully perform are bodily indeed, but the thought which animates them takes my body to be one thing and my act to be a total effect. I am concerned with what I, the animal person, do, not with the constituent activities of those minute parts in and through which my animal person has its being. If, then, the parallel is to be drawn at all strictly, with God's will the mind of the Universe as I am the mind of my body, then the action which concerns the divine will must be the action of the whole, not the actions of the multitudinous constituent parts in which the whole subsists. We shall be back again by another route to a modified Aristotelianism; God's thought will govern the grand movement of the universe, a movement which employs the constituent movements, but is unconcerned with them except as *conditiones sine quibus non* for its majestic gyrations.

'Not Aristotle again! Whichever way we turn, we are confronted by that tedious ghost. Would it not be better if we resolved to ignore him, and to pursue the question on its merits? I am not much impressed, I must say, by the point you have just brought forward. "If," you say, "the parallel is to be drawn at all strictly." But surely it cannot be drawn so strictly as to saddle the deity with every limitation of our finitude. Human intention shows its finite scope by going no further into the detail of its own action than a grasp of the macroscopic effect requires. It must be our hypothesis that the Universal Mind is infinite; it goes to the bottom of detail, it wills the total action through and through.'

I am happy to agree with you. All I want is to see the necessary qualifications made, and you have introduced one that is certainly vital. There are more yet to come, however. You suggest that we might speak of God's will as though it were purpose animating a body so comprehensively as to penetrate the minutest detail of being or of action which goes to the make-up of it; the 'body' in this case being the universe. Very well. But to talk like this is still to take one's start from the great totality and work down into the detail; and that again is to take it for granted that there really is a totality—a totality, I mean, which adds up to some sort of vital unity. Were there no dominant system of vital functions in my body for my mind to be the mind of, my mind would lose its physical setting and I should not know what could be meant by calling it the mind of this body. My body is an organism; to all evidence, the universe is no such thing.

The difficulty I am raising is familiar in connexion with the traditional 'Argument from Design'. It is a shockingly rash and careless presentation of the case which claims that the universe is a designed whole. Only it seems easier to save that Argument than it is to save your thesis. The Argument may still have some force if it abates its pretensions, and points simply to elements of design (if any such there be) not plausibly traceable to the action of natural forces unaided. Your claim that the universe is an organic whole, such as to supply God's will with a 'body', is, as an allegation, more staggeringly false even than the claim that it is a total design. What is worse, your claim does not allow of modification or abatement, it is all or nothing. Elements of organisation here or there among the galaxies will not help to save it in any form.

'This is not fair. The Argument from Design is an argument. I never dreamt of arguing from the superorganic structure of the sum of things to a Mind of the Universe. On the contrary, I accepted by way of hypothesis your own basis of reasoning, your conventional inference to a First Cause, a Primal Determinant, a free and sovereign Will. I merely ventured to help you over the puzzle, how to conceive the joint (as it were) between the action of the universal Will, and the actions of finite agents whether voluntary or merely natural. And I said that we could scarcely do otherwise than follow the model our own being provides—a relation between a rational organic agency and the cellular agencies it organises. Now you appear to be saying that I have no right to apply the model unless the sovereign mind's concern for the whole takes precedence over his concern for the actions of the constituent parts; and that this can scarcely be so unless the universe appears to be a whole in a more than trivial sense; to be, indeed, the organism of all organisms.

'If that is your contention, then I reject it. Did not we agree in attributing to our finitude the incarnation of our own mind or will in a single level of organising pattern? Once we have admitted an infinite Mind, embracing all detail and penetrating every level, why should we make it a matter of principle that it should be any more yoked to the action of the whole, than to that of the part? We have no interest in falsifying the balance of the universe; let it be whatever it appears to be—no organism, if you like, but a loose society, of which the organised activity is centred in the parts rather than in the whole. The distribution of the divine volition may correspond to the distribution of cosmic action, whatever that may be.'

You will scarcely expect me to quarrel with you, when you so obligingly move in the direction I want you to take. What I wonder is, once we have gone so far, how much substance there remains in the analogy you originally proposed. But before we can decide that issue, we have still further to go on the road we have been travelling.

You declare your readiness to admit the apparent balance between whole and part in the universe, and to accept the verdict of scientific observation. But suppose the verdict of scientific observation to be, that there neither is nor can be any such thing as a universal whole. Then what becomes of your balance? You cannot hold a balance between the real and the fictitious, still less between the intelligible and the nonsensical.

And the universe is not a whole. The cosmic paradoxes of space and time should have convinced us. No one denies that the human mind can place whatever it knows or comprehends of cosmic fact in a single generalised diagram; but the real order of things is diagrammatisable, not diagrammatic; the diagrammatic unity is in the mind, not in the world. It is nothing but the great Newtonian fiction of a space-time continuum viewed from no point in space and from no moment in time. It was shown up for what it was almost as soon as Newton had defined it; Leibniz wrote it off as the *phenomenon bene fundatum*. Realities do not coexist by absolute position in a Newtonian continuum; they coexist by constituting a field of conditions for any single piece of organised agency. The universe is indeed organised, or drawn together into unity; but it is so organised or drawn together a million million times over at all the single points where a field of forces finds a focus; and that is wherever any single active existence is present. All of these focal points have a certain extension—they are patterns of activity. Our own sentient animal existence is a highly-developed example. But to all evidence, there is no world-pattern pulling the universe together; it is pulled together by each of the infinite overlapping multitude of focal patterns, the patterns of actual and active existences.

If that is so—and to the best of our knowledge it is so—what can this analogy of yours do except mislead? Thought and purpose in a man animate or direct a pattern of action which organises and, as it were, builds upon a multitude of cellular activities. There is no such organising pattern on the cosmic scale, so how can the universal will bear upon us and our fellow-creatures in any way significantly analogous? If the God of Nature pulls the universe together, he must be presumed to do it through his creative employment of the energies which do pull the universe together. And these, as we have seen, are nothing but the individual 'creatures' in their focal capacity.

'It is not easy to counter what you say, so long as we are tailoring our theology to fit our natural philosophy. But one learns prudence, even in philosophising; and experience of the game should have taught us that just when theology has been trimmed down to a perfect fit with natural fact, the theology vanishes. It is not surprising; for the theistic postulation, even when it is made in answer to questions posed by the world of nature, demands belief in a reality which is itself non-natural, the divine. In any settlement of boundary-issues between God and nature, there must be give-and-take; the divine has its own logic and must be allowed its own rights. It is as vital that God should remain God, as that nature should remain nature.

'If, then, God is to be God, it may be necessary to postulate schemes of divine action in or upon nature, which are not visible in the pattern of natural events as they are naturally interpreted by us. The notion of a world-form organising the million million constituents, may be such a necessary postulate. Who indeed can doubt that it is so? Who that is ready to entertain the idea of God at all can be content to limit his action in the way you appear to suggest? Is God simply to support each of nature's constituents in being itself? Shall he do nothing to unify the whole otherwise than it is unified by the action of each constituent in drawing the field of environing forces into its focus?

Then the action of God simply reduces to the action of nature; and the claim that the action of natural forces is divinely willed reduces to the statement that they act. Every theist of any kind wants, surely, to say that natural activities or processes are placed by divine wisdom in some general scheme, a scheme transcending any built-in self-orientation of their own, and proper to the scope of a divine agent.'

I agree, of course, with the substance of what you say. The divine must have its rights or there will be no theology. Divine thought must comprehend the whole. Divine intention must extend more widely than the immediate functioning of each agency among the many constitutive of nature. None of this is in dispute. The question is, how all of it can be asserted in a form which best allows nature to be natural or, if you like, adds to nature working extensions least out of keeping with what we know of her. The action of a cosmic superorganism is a very violent hypothesis, which fits none of our scientific or other natural knowledge; and we have no need to suppose anything of the kind, since a less extravagant supposition is open to us.

If we want light on the divine mind's covering the world, we turn inevitably to our own mind's covering of it. As we were observing, we cannot get the cosmos into our heads except in the artificial diagram of a neutral continuum. On a smaller scale, however, we can proceed more realistically. If we are merely considering the coexistence of a limited number of our sentient fellow-creatures, we can adopt the standpoint of each in turn and, while we do so, see the others as constituting his field or environment. That, if you like, is an artificial exercise. But when we are in discourse or in personal relation with our fellows, we see simultaneously from their centre and from our own by the mere fact of taking their meaning; for their meaning is what *they* intend, it is not a theorem of our own thought.

Now agreeable as it often is simply to appreciate and sympathetically to enjoy the active existence of our fellow-beings, the aim of mutual understanding is commonly more practical. Our object is harmonisation, co-operation, common enrichment of life; in a word, society. Social aims are entertained in some measure by the most selfish; and they unquestionably extend beyond the natural objectives of individuals singly regarded. On the other hand, the social frame is not a super-organism; to take it as such has been the tragic error of philosophical thought, a mistake not merely academic, but carrying political implications nothing short of disastrous.

What we in fact think of the divine will in its application to ourselves is that its extension is a social extension. We take it that the divine purpose is to achieve our individual good through social action and mutual concern. And when we look behind our existence and see the divine will as having placed or created us, we take that will to be animated by a social providence. If God meant to make an individual person, he cannot have intended him without intending the society he would form with others; for apart from that he could not have been himself.

To give value to the providence of God there is no need to make the universe out to be *a* society, let alone the society of societies, normative of all others. It is enough to say that God, knowing each of his creatures from within its action, and viewing its world from the standpoint of its being, cares for such mutual harmonisations of natural agents as are necessary to the existence or the development of the creatures he creates. Here is a theme on which one might endlessly enlarge, and I have indeed expatiated on it elsewhere; especially in comment on the patience (as it were) of the creative Wisdom in achieving his combined effects without forcing the limited and often brutal principles of activity native to the several agents he employs; a patience which shows itself in the toleration of much that we call waste, chaos and disaster.

The theme belongs to another occasion. We are considering the proper and improper applications of the analogy embodied in the formula, 'God, or the divine thought, is the mind of the world.' And after so much urged against improper applications, it is time that something was said about the proper way to take it. God is the mind of the world—Yes, indeed, and that is how he differs from my mind which can never be more than the mind of me. True, I attempt to enter into the subjectivity of a limited number among my fellow-beings, but my power to do so is very imperfect; and even then I cannot become their mind, so as to cause or operate their proper action; it is theirs, not mine. But God is the Mind *of the World*, that is, he is not tied to any base of operation that is exclusively his; he enters fully into the subjectivity of all the world's constituents. What is more, he does not enter into them simply after the event, with a sympathy perfect, perhaps, but still impotent; he enters into them by prior causality, willing them the existence and the activity they exercise; and so he is indeed *the Mind* of the world.

So much for a brief statement of the force attaching to the analogy. It will be seen that it takes as its foundation the heights our mental activities aspire to reach, not the limitations they endure. It virtually amounts to a statement of transcendence and of first causality. To be the mind not merely of you or of me but of all creatures, God must be a free Spirit, whose action is prior to the actions of them all. Such being the value of the analogy, it is clear that it casts no light whatever on the mysterious causal joint between prime agency (the Creator's) and second agency (the creature's); a relation which it simply presupposes. God's being the mind of the world does nothing towards identifying his action with that of an organic whole, to which the actions of the cellular constituents are geared.

'Well, but surely the divine mind may be allowed to confer unity on the universe by embracing it in his own single and infinitely multiform activity.'

Yes, of course; the statement is true in so far as it is tautological. By concerning himself with a plurality he unites it in the unity of his concern. The unity is the unity of the divine initiative. Only, in making even so innocent a statement as this, we need to be on our guard against the false suggestions of the human model. When a man confers a sort of unity on a miscellaneous collection of persons, animals and objects by giving them a place in his multifarious activities or interests, he does impose upon them a scheme of order which is his own, and alien to them. For the possible patterns of human interest or activity, though indefinitely numerous, remain specifically human. However varied, they are variations on set themes. Whereas it would surely be irrational to suppose in God a determinate nature, like that of a finite species, prescribing an order in his concern with things particular to himself and foreign to the things. Surely his concern for his creatures is for them to be themselves, or more than themselves; not for them to act as pawns in some specifically supernatural game which any divine hand is bound to play. A man's concern for his fellow-beings, however generous, must be a straitjacket compared with the openness of God's concern for the world.

CHAPTER XI

INCORPOREAL SPIRIT

IT was said by the most successful theological apologist our days have seen, that never was his sense of a truth so weak as when he had just successfully vindicated it. The experience is common, and the psychology not difficult to divine. We ourselves have just piled reason on reason in disproof of *anima mundi* theology. Were not the reasons good? Yet the position they demolished seems to stand entire. Perhaps we did not let the strength of the defence find a voice. Let us try again; and, as our custom is, let us give the floor to our critic.

'Metaphysical truth,' he says, 'may be ideally speaking timeless, but the formulations in which we approximate to it have a strong period colour. When we have the feeling that such-and-such a doctrine can no longer be held in the mid twentieth century, we ought not to act on that feeling without reflection; we ought, nevertheless, to take it as a serious invitation to reflect. Have you not an uneasy feeling that an orthodox doctrine of divine transcendence has an old-world air about it? If you have, may I venture to point out to you two good reasons why you should think so?

'First, you have been purging out the Aristotelian leaven, but even now you have not made a job of it. As you told us, Aristotle's doctrine of causes put being before becoming, and so, ascending step by step the causal stair, came to a first being exempt from all becoming, a pure living essence who simply was. That the sheerest transcendence fits in such a picture, who can doubt? It did not take St Thomas many lines to demolish those who made the Aristotelian Absolute incarnate in the astral sphere. But your causal story is not the Aristotelian story. You go back from part-determined acts to acts part-determining them, till you reach an undetermined, purely determining act. Such an Act is clearly not related to bodily being as my voluntary action is related to mine, for he has the entire mastery of what he governs, and makes it what he will. But that is not to say that he is independent of it or has any action otherwise than in determining it. Why should a free Creator, however free, exist otherwise than in freely creating?

'And now I come to the second reason. It is not only that the Aristotelian prop is knocked away from sheer transcendence; it is that pure spirit has become unthinkable to us. Nothing has been more decisively secured by philosophical reflection in our time, than a clearer view of the relation between mind and body. The pretence of reducing intentional action to physical event remains, indeed, the folly it always was; but the suggestion that any mental act could dispense with a physical instrument or vehicle has been exploded. Thought is not physical process, because thought is meaning, and no physical process qua physical is a meaning. All meaning nevertheless is the meaning of some physical act performed with that meaning; even though the physical act be as slight as an interior flicker of the nerves showing no outward sign but experienced, it may be, as silent speech or mental imaging. Meanings are carried by acts and those acts are employments of bodily powers, however subtle, however refined. That any thought should detach itself from its instrument is not so much a wild improbability as a logical monstrosity. And so the Christian philosophers of our time, when they think about the destiny of the soul, are happy to lean on the old biblical hope of bodily resurrection—that if we are to receive a life hereafter from the hand of omnipotence, it will be through a renewed instrument, a 'spiritual body', taking over the rhythms and registrations of the perished body in such a way (God knows how) as to preserve a personal continuity.

'What, then, are we to think of Divine Mind? Can we meaningfully cut it away from every bodily basis? To judge sensibly about the question, we may usefully recur to the rock-bottom of theistic reflection, as we outlined it some pages back. The theist has always been the man who, seeing that nature is not the effect of natural decision, acknowledges supernatural will. In pagan times the god was a dominant constituent among the constituents of the universe; he was localised in an immortal body. Deeper reflection, seeking in God the universal Cause, was precluded from tying him to a particular organisation of matter. How, then, was his being to be conceived? A false spiritualism in the theory of mind-as-such offered an easy solution; God was pure spirit or simple mind, free of those paradoxical ties which were seen as anchoring mind to body in us.

'Such was the orthodoxy of close on two thousand years. It has now to be set aside as an aberration. We know nothing of separate or separable mind. A contemporary reflection on God's manner of existence should take the form of a speculation on the unique tie between God and material events. For though the tie is not to be denied, it must evidently be unique. It cannot restrict his thought to the intelligent action of a particular organism, in downright pagan fashion; it cannot correlate him with the superorganism of the universe, since, as you have pointed out, the universe is not a superorganism, nor, indeed, a totality which exists as such at all. But it is surely in the worst tradition of metaphysical debate to conclude that there is no third alternative; and that if God has neither a body within the world nor a world-body, his mental action dwells in no bodily action whatever.

'We are admittedly talking metaphysics, and so we shall be employing "stretched" conceptions in any case. The vice of metaphysical argument is to reject your opponent's positions because they involve the stretching of natural terms, while overlooking or disguising the equally stretched senses implicit in your own. It is plain enough that the embodiment of the divine action will have to be "embodiment" in a stretched sense. But before we conclude that there is therefore no embodiment of it, we should take note that by concluding so we shall be left with our notions not less, but more stretched than they were. For we shall be asserting the existence of personal action, or of active personality, in a form quite unknown to us, the totally disembodied.

'All this, I recognise, is mere preliminary skirmishing. The substance of my case must lie in the positive account I am ready to offer of the relation I wish to maintain. I will present you with no wire-drawn artificialities; I will follow the natural line of theistic reflection, to acknowledge a creative will behind the action of every finite agent. Whatever we may think of the life of God in God, we are obliged to admit his action in his creatures, apart from which we should know nothing of him. Transcendence or no transcendence, we have to wrestle with the paradox: two agencies of different level taking effect in the same finite action, the finite agency which lives in it, the infinite agency which founds it. On any theistic hypothesis, such founding action is a mode of God's active existence; and what reason have we to suppose any other mode of it?

'The physical action in which the action of God's mind or will dwells need therefore be accounted no other than the action of each and every creature. Mind, as we have said, is the enjoyed meaning with which any meaningful action is done. On the theistic hypothesis, everything that is done in this world by intelligent creatures is done with two meanings: the meaning of the creature in acting, the meaning of the Creator in founding or supporting that action. Subjectively considered, there are two doings; physically there is but one event. Where the creature concerned is non-intelligent there are not two meanings, for only the Creator has a meaning or intention. But there are still two doings; it is the act of the Creator that the creature should either act or be there to act. Ought we not to say that it is in creative doing that the Creative Mind both thinks and exists? Since it is nonsensical to suppose a beginning of the Creator, we shall take it that he has always been creatively engaged upon material realities; the physical world has always been. And why not? It is an easier thing to conceive than an absolute beginning of physical time, or in physical time.

'There is obviously much that would need to be said in

development of the doctrine; but I am content to leave it with you for the present as I have stated it. The strength of it lies in its broadest principles. It should not be beyond us to adjust it to the detailed applications that may be called for.'

You are certainly persuasive; and yet my mind misgives me. I agree with you that what theistic reflection comes to assert is the prior decisiveness of the divine will, rather than any particular theory of the way in which that will subsists; and so it is open to you to speculate on the manner of its subsistence. But I doubt whether your attempt to give body to the divine act really amounts to anything. You say very truly that the theistic hypothesis involves the assertion of two meanings carried by every finite activity: the meaning for the finite agent, and the meaning for the infinite Creator. Or rather, if we are to be exact, meaning for the finite agent is only present in so far as that agent is capable of meaning anything by what he does. The higher animals may be credited with meaning; at lower levels there is a sort of blind persistence in the exercise of function which (to our imaginations) does duty for it. Meaning, for the agent, is proportioned to the scope of alternative action, the capacity for controlled imaging, the mechanism of linguistic symbolisation, etc. To say that thought and decision have a bodily basis is not simply to say that they are carried by physical acts of some kind; it is to say that they are possible uses of the physical acts they employ.

But what are we to say about the relation between divine thought or decision and the physical action which, according to your hypothesis, is somehow to carry it? The action (which is the existence) of the finite agent means something to its creator, as well as to itself. So far the formula is acceptable. But how much does it mean? Is what it means to the Creator limited by the natural capacities of the physical instrument, as what it can mean to the agent is limited? Surely not, for then the Creator cannot see an inch ahead of the creature and the creative mind becomes an idle hypothesis. Shall we not want to say that the creature's action means to the Creator its place in its whole context, both actual and projected? But if so, how can it be said to act as the bodily vehicle for all this meaning? If any physical action, even the slightest and the most elementary, can mean the universe, its relation to the meaning it carries becomes purely accidental. If any act you like can be the vehicle of any meaning you like, it is no longer the vehicle of it.

In fact, this whole line of talk is revealed as the product of equivocation. I can say very reasonably that, did we but know, some very slight physical event *means* a vast complex of physical activities; but when I say this, I am supposing human observers, equipped with their own cerebral machinery; it is to them that (in the ideal case) the event in question would mean all this; and then they would not get the meaning in a flash; it might cost them much time and many movements of thought before they could possess themselves of it. I should never want to say that a simple physical event stands *to itself* as a symbol of its total context or that, by merely occurring, it possesses all that truth. It is (I submit) nonsensical to say that the occurrence of a simple physical event carries or constitutes a divine thought embracing the universe. What we want to say is that from the focus of that event divine wisdom can read the universe of events. But that is because divine wisdom, so far from being embodied in that event, transcends all events utterly.

'As I listened to you I was wondering why I felt your criticism to be shooting beside the mark; your last phrase gives you away. You are not talking natural theology; you are expounding religious dogmatism. It may be consoling to faith, to believe an almighty Omniscience; it is not evident that cool reflection upon natural fact suggests it. I agree that theism is an idle hypothesis unless the divine will has a real priority and keeps the lead over finite existences; for it is nothing if it is not the determinant of their occurrence. But is it not sufficient to see each act of that will as limited (since after all its matter of concern is limited)? May not it be—as it were—the personified demand of the given situation, looking out its next phase? When I make the physical event the vehicle of a divine meaning in addition to any meaning it may carry for itself, I have no notion of loading it with omniscience.'

I see. But I cannot feel that your concession really helps the difficulty. Let us remember that in the vast spread of the universe higher organisms are an extreme rarity. Where they are absent, you will have to see the Creative Will as incarnate in the very simplest physical processes or acts. And I shall have to insist that, since such acts have no natural aptitude to be the vehicles of a forward-ranging thought or decision, their acting as such is far less intelligible than a burst into speech on the part of Balaam's ass; and really presupposes an existent Wisdom, who chooses to confer upon his instruments a function for which they have no natural serviceableness. And then, why should he? The God of Balaam might make the ass talk as a way of getting at her master. What motive the God of the atoms could have for pinning prescience on them, I cannot conceive.

When we were boys, we read Bergson and Whitehead. We understood Whitehead to tell us that, supposing the validity of universal principles in the natural world, it was still necessary to postulate a 'principle of concretion' to explain the particular combinations constituting brute-fact. But reading Whitehead with benevolence, we did not accuse him of making his 'principle of concretion' the description of a real being, agency or force. He was saying that a determinant so acting in the natural world must be supposed; the character of that determinant itself would be a further question, a properly metaphysical enquiry. Here again was Bergson, postulating a forward-groping endeavour on the part of an *élan vital* in biological species, not to be limited to the purposefulness of individuals, nor accounted for by it. We gave him, too, the benefit of the doubt—he could not, surely, suppose that he was describing a being or agency, but merely a seeming effect; to decide how the agent of it ought rightly to be conceived, would be a question for hard metaphysical debate. So, when you in turn tell me that the natural facts suggest to a first reflection no more than a reaching forward of creative will out of the existing situation towards a next phase, I do not quarrel with you. I merely ask you to consider how meaningless it is to make the present phase of physical action the bodily vehicle of that creative thought.

'Perhaps there is no need for us to interpret Whitehead or Bergson. It is task enough, to keep our own discussion on the rails. My reaction to your latest criticism is to protest against such an atomisation of the divine thinking as it implies. Why am I expected to agree that the single created event in isolation and apart from all others is charged with the load of divine meaning? Who that believed in God at all could doubt that all created realities are willed together by him? No one can suppose that the single physical act, or phase of process, is the vehicle of his thought. Whereas all the events in the universe, seen as enacted by the Creative Intention, are sufficient, surely, to give body to the Creative Mind.'

In a certain sense no orthodox thinker would wish to dispute what you say. It is conventional to hold that God's creative thought is both perfectly effective and perfectly economical. It employs no scaffolding of supposition, argument, or tentative proposal but goes straight to the mark of what it creates. The things, in their actuality, are the thoughts of him for whom to think is to do. But the unity or focus of the divine thought is just God himself. I must recur to my previous point—the universe is not a unity; it does not exist, even, as any sort of whole. And since it is the unity of the thoughts attaching to the several minute creaturely facts which allows them to be thought at all, or anyhow to be thought divinely, it seems senseless to make a physical plurality which affords that unity no basis, a body of which God is the mind.

One of the strongest motives behind the several forms of that protean phenomenon which I call *anima mundi* theology is the desire to bring the divine life into the stream of time. Aristotle saw the divine act as the effortless possession of timeless truth; a changeless enjoyment which might be called Mind by courtesy, but Person by no stretch of terms. His Christian disciples were bound to qualify the doctrine, since the God of the Bible and of the Church created by free decision and intervened by particular initiative. They stood it out nevertheless that the world-directed acts of God were events in the creature only, their roots in the divine will being utterly timeless. The compromise is scarcely intelligible and, if intelligible at all, depersonalising. And it seems the downright and effective remedy, to admit that God simply does live the history of the world, in some sense analogous to the way in which I live the history of my body, though from a position of infinitely more effective sovereignty.

One cannot fail to sympathise with the anti-scholastic revolt; and it seems fair to say that if we attribute to God a life of creative volition we shall see his acts under the temporal form, not only in their effect, but in God's living of them. But it is absurd to say that we in this world have got all the time there is, and if God wants any of it, he will have to come in and have a bit of ours. There is no such thing as time; there is activity, which viewed objectively, may be called process; and there are relations of before and after within it, which for various purposes may be abstracted, described and diagrammatised in various ways. The time-relations to be found within process are determined by the structure of the process, not *vice versa*; if we knew what it was like to be God, or to live the life of God, we should know what there is in his existence analogous to the temporal forms which characterise ours. But perhaps we shall not be so rash as to claim that knowledge.

No doubt there is a deceptive simplicity about the suggestion, that if God acts in our world he is in one time-order with us; but as we see when we examine it, the proposition makes no sense. Nothing can be in our time-order without being a natural constituent of our world.

The universe is a unity in time only in the sense that every event or act is linked to every other either directly or indirectly by temporal chains. A time-series runs through every several train of process leading up to a given phase of that process; and equally through every train of circumstance, or of exterior cause, seen as impinging upon or conditioning it. There may be no time-series relating the event A to the event B, but it will always be possible to find, or to hope for, an event C which will be related temporally to both of them. The universe is not a process, but a tissue of processes without number; it has no history, therefore, but is (as it were) a complex of interlocked biographies. If there is a divine knower, he can know all there is to know about the many series of successions in the universe by enjoying individually the points of view proper to all phases of process. But he can do so only because he is not himself at any time.

It is no doubt a very foolish piece of theology which makes the time-transcendent mode of God's being a bar against his entering into the temporeity of his creatures' existences by his knowledge of them or his action in them. The first capacity of the infinite is to fill every finitude. But it is a folly no less extreme to think that we bring God and his creatures together by attaching our temporal conditions to his existence. Is God to enrich his experience as he goes forward in developing the world-process? How can he, when there is no world-process nor any world-time? We cannot ask 'Where has God got to with the Universe at the present moment?' We cannot rule a date-line across the galaxies and ask how things look to the Almighty on the first of June in the current year. Things are doubtless in their own temporal orders to him, because he sees them as they are. Their Creator is concerned to get each of them through the narrow gate of its own next moment, an aperture fixed and outlined for it by all the trains of event converging upon it. No such moment, no such gate confronts his own existence; unless indeed he is a mere constituent of the world himself, like the Apollo or Neptune of old mythology.

You can say if you like that every thought of God concerning a creature, and every act of God in a creature, has temporal form for God. What you scarcely can want to say is that all such acts or thoughts as he desires to make queue up for their turn of being his thought or his act. If you establish temporal dimension within each of his acts, you still cannot establish a temporal order among his acts. Consider, then, a mind or will capable of an infinity of acts without limitation of temporal order amongst them. How can you say that such a mind is geared to the temporal processes it rules? Whether we look at what we know of the world, or whether we look at what we must think of God, the conclusion is the same. The world is not such, that God could be said to live its history under the form of one time; God is not such, that his life can be confined within temporal dimensions. If he is to animate and visit his creatures, it must be out of his transcendence.

'What you say has some force, but it is the force of a well-known and inconclusive procedure. You work up the paradoxes involved in an attempt to relate God and the world in any practical or imaginable manner and make them an excuse for placing his being in a cloud of mystery and at an inconceivable distance. Between the unintelligibilities of positive paradox and of vacuous negation one might find little to choose, and I for my part have no wish to join you in swinging the metaphysical seesaw on that issue. Allow me to carry you back to the point from which we started. I wanted to know, and I still want to know, whether after all that has been discovered or thought in the last century or so, you propose to make the being of God mere mind?'

I do not; I propose to acknowledge in him sheer act. Thought, in the human creature, is a specialised phase of heedful action, separated (because of our limited powers of attention) from that full-blooded and efficacious action to which it normally conduces. Doubtless God acts intelligently and understands actively, without separation of functions.

I wonder whether you have sufficiently examined the grounds of your prejudice against disembodied act? Body is taken by sense to be sheer crass material. But neither science, nor a philosophy scientifically enlightened, can uphold that view. The bottom of substance is ceaseless act. To say that, with us, mind is embodied, is to say that our personal action is geared to the working of many minute actions themselves organising actions yet more minute. And naturally, for our personal action is one arising out of the world; it is not, like God's, that out of which the world arises. His action, being prior and creative, is free and simple. Surely, to believe in God is to believe exactly this.

If we deny the possibility of disembodied action, physicists may laugh at us, for the basic energy of the world, whatever it is, is not embodied in anything. What we cannot conceive is action *in vacuo*, that is, action without interplay. But to Christians at least it has not appeared that the Godhead self-disclosed to them exhibits so desolating and inconceivable a solitude. They believe Trinity of Persons in Unity of Substance.

'It requires some assurance on the part of a theologian to put forward the Trinity in a philosophical discussion; but let it pass, for whatever we are discussing, we are not discussing that. What I prefer to contest is your allegation that "the prejudice in favour of bodiliness" is simply the child of uncriticised sense. Physical being has the advantage of permanence, however purely active it may be; personal existence as we know it is a transitory flash. Through its embodiment it finds a brief footing on ground that everlastingly endures; to our knowledge there is no beginning and no end of physical action in the universe. To think of God is to think of everlasting will. What more reasonable, then, than to see in him a personal existence overcoming that transitoriness which in ourselves we deplore, and obtaining an unshakeable grasp on the whole extent of physical being?

'The contention cannot be met by simply protesting that in the view of Christian believers the human soul is immortal; not, that is, unless our immortality is asserted as intrinsic to us. If it is the gift of God, and a gratuitous transformation of our nature, it cannot be made the ground for a claim that what we are fits us to be the types of God's eternity. It will remain that our personal being is a momentary thing, in face of the enduring matter of the world.'

No; the proper way to deal with the argument is not to deify the soul; it is to liquidate the matter. Perhaps the continuance of the universe is guaranteed rather by a rule of replacement than by any ultimate permanence of constituents. Nevertheless I suppose that many of these constituents, atomic or molecular, outlast a thousand thousand human lives. But what does their lastingness mean? A pattern of activity persists in cyclic iteration. What are we to say of the unity through time of what persists? At any moment we can say that the dying phase is, as it were, the parent of the living phase to which it bequeathes form and direction. That parent-phase had a parent-phase behind it, and so *ad infinitum*. But only the immediately past phase is dynamically present in the passing phase by the fact of shaping it. The previous phases of repeating process are mere history, lost and irrecoverable by the present phase. It can strike no root back into the deeper past. It is our minds which follow back the causal trail, and diagrammatise the succession of perishing instants by a line of coexistent continuous parts.

When we consider an extended history of human ancestry, we are immediately struck by its discontinuity; it consists not of the life of a family, but of the lives of men. In moralising vein we may contrast the brief tenure of successive heirs with the agelong permanence of the acres they inherit. The molecules composing the stones in their fields outlast a hundred generations. The comparison is more striking than philosophical. There is as firm a continuity of physical process running through the tree of ancestry as through the persistence of the molecule. What parcels out the family descent is not a comparative absence of unity but a comparative surplus of it. Each living heir achieves a sort of unity-through-time of which no part of the molecule process is for one moment capable. And so the family process is drawn together into successive overlapping unities which by their intensity of focussing power exclude one another. Even then the exclusion is not in every sense absolute: a man's active existence may strike roots into his ancestry in so far as he embraces a cherished tradition, and lives by it; or, indeed, consciously revolts against it.

When theistic reasoning puts God behind the world it is going back from a crumbling multiplicity to some unitary firmness. To conceive the eternity of God by analogy with a continuous succession of mere perishing phases in simple iteration is a very feeble and inappropriate piece of imaginaging. We do not need to load the human person with that immortality it hopes from the hand of God, in order to make it our nearest image of God's eternity. No other agent that we know pulls together or grasps in one any extent or content of existence.

George Berkeley overplayed his hand when, to establish the throne of Spirit, he abolished physical matter. It is enough if we pulverise that idol of the mind, the universe. What we call by that name is a map, a diagram of our construction, true in the main as diagrams are true, and serviceable for finding our way among those live points of process in which alone the world is actual. Even the name 'map' is dangerous, for the correctness of a map is taken to entail the simultaneous extended actuality of the area it symbolises. 'The Universe' is more like a linear diagram of historical developments, chalked on a classroom blackboard. The usefulness of the drawing does not suppose the coexistence of the complex it refers to.

Our simple theist, with whom we began, knows himself as a being both posited and self-positing. Looking for the simply self-positing positor, he cannot see him in his fellows, still less in his inferiors; he looks above his own head. He is perfectly philosophical, whether he knows it or not. The universe of our acquaintance contains no other possible clue beside the upward orientation of our personal actuality.

It is time to strike the balance of discussion. It has not, perhaps, been held level. The difficulties of theistic semi-naturalism, or *anima mundi* theology, have been exposed; the paradoxes besetting transcendentalism have not been equally probed. The transcendentalist may hope to have refuted the rash claim that the relation of created activities to the Creative Act can be made closely analogous to a natural relation, and in so far intelligible. He has not in so doing shown the absolute untenability of what he would call half-theologies, or removed their attractiveness for minds whose religious attitude they fit or form. It often becomes evident to the orthodox student of such systems that their authors are simply articulating a strange religion. The God of Professor Hartshorne, for example, must be human enough to have a natural need of his creatures. It is apparently a matter of no concern that he should be divine enough to save their souls alive. Here is a rival doctrine about that divine charity which is the heart of our religion. The fervour of the faith behind the teaching is unmistakeable; it claims to be judged as a new revelation, not as a rational conclusion.

If our discussion had in fact established an orthodox doctrine of transcendence, it would have been beyond the purpose of so slight an essay. Our thesis is no more than that the relation of created act to creative Act is inevitably indefinable, and that its being so is neither an obstacle to religion, nor a scandal to reason.

CHAPTER XII

THE ARGUMENT IN SUMMARY

I. THE BELIEVER'S REASONS

Theism is a standing belief which, if rightly held, must presumably be held on sound motives somewhere. A philosopher should begin by examining actual and acknowledged motives with patience.

The substance of the belief derives from age-old tradition; it continues to hold us by the force of present motives. The genuine believer is a judge of good and bad motives for faith. He may philosophise poorly, or not at all, about the underlying supposition on which all faith-motives operate. The philosopher should lay bare that supposition and examine its validity. The examination is bound to carry him into metaphysical depths.

II. THE EMPIRICAL DEMAND

If life-in-faith is taken as providing evidence of God, the philosopher will ask whether the evidence can satisfy empirical criteria of objectivity. Not physical criteria, evidently. Is there any conceivable refinement of the empirical principle which does not bar theology *ab initio*? We propose the formula 'We can think about no reality, about which we can do nothing but think', and proceed to consider in what sense we are said to 'do anything' about God.

Shall we say that we worship him? But what is it to worship? It is shown that the most contemplative adoration rests upon a practical relation of our action to the divine.

III. SPIRITUAL SCIENCE

If we call our relation to God one of mutually engaged activities, we appear to bring it under a generic description. In fact we cannot pretend to do more than place it in a suggested analogy. Analogy with what? With personal or with natural relation? It is possible to argue for the latter. Are not the activities that bear on us from the divine side spiritual forces or gracious influences, which affect us causally, or condition us? And is not their action to some extent predictable? It may be so; but a mere susceptibility to such forces cannot be the ground of belief in transcendent deity. Only an experience in a form analogous to personal dealing with some other can carry conviction of that other's self-being.

IV. GRACE AND FREEWILL

We accordingly examine the analogy between friendship and religion and ask whether it will support the claim that theistic evidence is 'empirical'. Only in a stretched sense, at the best. But what is the importance of the question? Empirical evidence, however exact, may be no sufficient ground for asserting *individual* existence. It is not the strength of evidence, but the necessity of valuation, that leads to such assertions.

Supposing an engagement of human with divine will, how do we conceive it? In practice, divine will is understood as purpose, recognised in its effect, and embraced by consent. How it wields creative agencies can never become a practical issue. The traditional problems of Grace and Freewill are simply expressions of the invisibility which covers the 'causal joint' between infinite and finite act.

V. NATURE AND CREATION

Active religion makes the theology of nature our practical concern; but it leaves our nature-theology free to go with the grain of natural fact.

As Kant saw, religious action gives us an interest in a positive answer to metaphysical questions left open by mere speculation. But he failed to give an adequate account of religious commitment. We are not committed to belief in an 'author of nature' by the contextual support which the belief gives to our free endeavours, but only by a life of direct relation with God.

There is a genuine parallel between the mysteriousness of (a) divine will underlying physical event and (b) divine will underlying human act. The parallel extends back to the moment of primary creation, a fact disguised by obsolete physical theories but now disclosed.

VI. REVELATION AND HISTORY

No theory of revelation is common to the great religions. We will examine the Christian doctrine, which Dr Richardson has usefully discussed. Is Revelation-History just history? Its matter is historical, its interpretative concepts are not simply so, for their reference is not to patterns of finite event alone; they refer to a transcendent agency.

Revealing history is in large part a history of revelations; of how events have been the will of God to men and have evoked their responses. But there is no firm line to draw between the revelatory and the responsive. The whole process is instrumental to God and the whole is flecked with creaturely imperfection. The paradox of double agency, creaturely and divine, is all-pervasive.

VII. THE THEOLOGY OF WILL

We have proposed two palliatives of our paradox: the inevitably 'analogical' nature of all statements about God, and the special unmanageableness of statements in areas not directly touching our action. The second palliative carries the positive obverse, that statements in the practical area must be manageable, and therefore not excessively paradoxical or analogical. The 'will of God' as 'what God does in the world' can, in fact, be literally conceived; not, however, its being God who wills it or does it. Will, nevertheless, remains our clearest indicator of the divine being itself. The God of religion is free, absolute, or sovereign Will.

Such a conception of the divine is equally proper in metaphysical speculation, as we show by a reform of the argument from contingency of being.

VIII. JUSTIFIABLE ANALOGY

'Necessary Being' and 'Unconditioned Will' each present logical difficulties, but difficulties not equally scandalous. 'Unconditioned Will' is the historical core of practical theism, and though irreducibly analogical, expresses the ideal terminus of human aspiration. What gives it actuality is a life lived in relation to it; the very form of such a life being belief in God, in the same sense as that in which belief in one's neighbours is the form of intercourse with them. But whereas life-with-men is integral to our personal being, and thus inescapably human, life-in-God is supernatural and so allows of being denied without self-stultification. Not that we believe in our neighbours *because* it is self-stultifying to deny their existence, but because we are involved with them; and such also is the cause of our belief in God.

IX. FIRST CAUSE

Once the habit is formed of seeking explanation for facts in natural causes, theology chases a nature-type causality back beyond nature into God. The Cartesians saw physical agents as no true causes and so could step back into a *contrasting* cause, Cosmic Mind or Will. We, like the Aristotelians, attribute real efficacy to physical agents, and so are tempted to physicalise the First Cause. The corrective is to take note of the inevitable anthropomorphy of all thought about agency or efficacy. A truly sufficient cause is *ipso facto* a super*human* agent. Aristotle derived the elements of causal doctrine from human action, but artificially logicised them. So he arrived at a First Cause which was not an Agent Will. And his error has endlessly misled Christian Europe.

X. ANIMA MUNDI

Though we have no concern with finding the 'causal joint' between divine agency and human, we must take the joint to exist, when we see our action as instrumental to the divine. We do think of it, therefore, and no doubt by some model or analogy. It is suggested that there is a close model in the control exercised by our voluntary activity over the minute constituents of our bodies. Is not the Divine Will the 'Soul of the World' and we individual creatures constituents in its 'body'? The analogy breaks down, however, because the Universe does not constitute an organic system, nor even exist as a totality. God can be the Universal Mind only by transcending that multiplicity which the Universe is.

XI. INCORPOREAL SPIRIT

Do we not, nevertheless, talk too easily about 'transcendence'? Have we not yet learned to regard discarnate mind as a logical monstrosity? And ought we to posit a God who is pure Spirit? Let the relation of creative act to created action be as mysterious as you like, ought we not to see the Creative Will as subsisting in the physical it creates? The hypothesis is examined, and the creatures found to be absurd vehicles of Universal Thought. A special difficulty for the hypothesis lies in the structure of the time-order.

We need not conceive God as discarnate thought, if that is mere meaning or naked idea. No, indeed; God is intelligent *act*.

XII. THE ARGUMENT IN SUMMARY

Our enquiry advances from the motives of faith to their underlying assumption. This being, that religious existence is an interaction with actual Godhead, religion challenges comparison with that active experience of our environment which yields 'empirical evidence'. Religious evidences are not, however, empirical in the same sense, because they do not touch the point of contact, or causal joint, between our action and the divine. The practical elusiveness of this joint can be studied in the fields of Grace, of Nature, and of Revelation. God is acknowledged simply as effective will, and must be conceived as unconditioned will: an idea as metaphysically as it is religiously acceptable. One might think that a theology of Will called for a metaphysic of immanence. But transcendentalism receives negative support from the inhospitality of the world we know towards a world-soul theology.